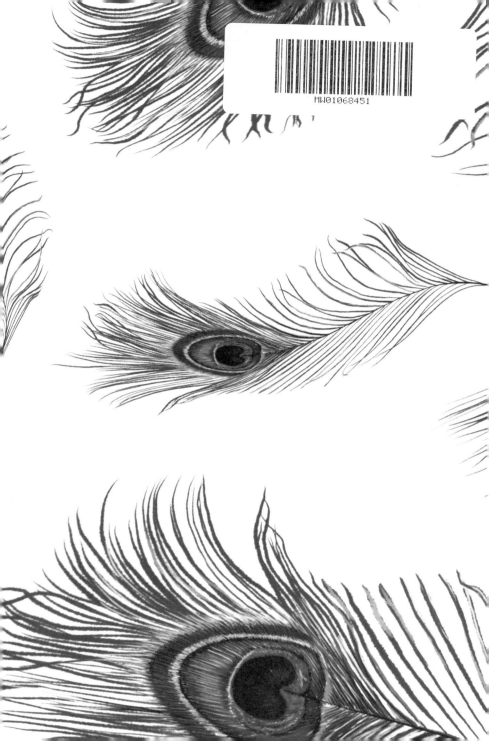

Praise for *Mysterion*

"The world is a gift: a sign and symbol of the Lord's love, created to convey to us the meaning of our own lives and the depths of God's goodness. In *Mysterion*, Fr. Ayre aims to point all Christians to that beautiful truth, and thus to invite us to a richer and more joyful relationship with Christ and his Church. Don't miss this book!"

— JD Flynn, Co-Founder of *The Pillar*

"Fr. Ayre wishes to challenge preconceptions we have about Christian living and to encourage us in areas of weakness. He does this by inviting us to embrace what he describes as a wide-ranging sacramental worldview and sharing his own experiences and reading. He succeeds admirably; readers will be grateful."

— Terrence Prendergast, S.J.,
Emeritus Archbishop of Ottawa-Cornwall

"Sacramentality is . . . what the world is begging for. [This is] the reality that our culture wants us to forget—that God is real, and everything has more meaning because of him. We do not live in this reality by adjusting to the world's standards, but by diving into the heart of the Church. Now is the time to bathe everything in our lives . . . in sacramentality. That's what Fr. Harrison is doing with this book."

— Luke Carey, Co-Host of *Catching Foxes* podcast

"Christ the Eternal Word expresses himself perfectly in the accessibility of human flesh. His accessibility loses nothing of his mystery; his mystery does not overwhelm his accessibility. Fr. Harrison's book, so needed today, opens the door to this vision; accessible and well expressed, as theology should be, it is a participation in the Incarnation."

— Bishop Daniel E. Flores, STD,
Bishop of Brownsville

"You will read this book with the eyes of reason and see the world through the eyes of faith, a world with God's grandeur pulsing through everything. It is imperative that this be read by all in Christ's body."

— Matthew John Paul Tan, Vianney College,
Diocese of Wagga Wagga

"The beginning of wisdom is fear of the Lord. From the gift of awe and wonder we can recover our love for the mystery of God celebrated in a liturgy that is true to the living tradition of the Church."

— Bishop Richard Umbers, Auxiliary Bishop of Sydney

"Fr. Ayre offers us a way of seeing. If we want to encounter God, he says, it cannot be as pure spirits: rather, it will be through the earthly and embodied world. The living God reveals himself in creation, and he reveals himself most profoundly in the Incarnation of Jesus Christ. To exist 'in Christ,' therefore, is to share sacramentally in Christ as members of his body; and so the *way of seeing* is a *way of living*. Read this eye-opening book to discover the pathways of a truly Catholic life!"

— Matthew Levering, James N. and Mary D. Perry Jr.
Chair of Theology, Mundelein Seminary

"Fr. Harrison's gift is the ability to make accessible the large ideas that we grapple with. *Mysterion: The Revelatory Power of the Sacramental Worldview* is no exception. I found myself drawn into the world of mystery by a hand that wants to share the sacramental worldview with love and passion. It reaches out to guide us to the very thing all Christians seek: how we should live to draw ever closer to God."

— Bonnie Landry, host of *Make Joy Normal* podcast

"This is a book of encounter. To read it is to rediscover oneself in a world alive to grace. We need theology like this: clear and deep, accessible and profound."

— Terence Sweeney, Collegium Institute for Catholic Thought & Culture and Villanova University Philosophy Department

"In *Mysterion*, Fr. Harrison Ayre's good pastoral sense and his theological aptitude come together in a tour de force that will open up new vistas in the faith life of any disciple. If the saints are those who have true vision, because they have seen the Lord, then Fr. Ayre's book helps us to see more as they do. This book will not only attune us more fully to Christ as he makes himself known to us, but also renew our appreciation and fervor for our life in him."

— Michael R. Heinlein, Editor of Our Sunday Visitor's *Simply Catholic*

"What does it mean to live in Christ and to see the world for what it really is—loved into being and redeemed from the inside out? Fr. Harrison Ayre's *Mysterion* is all encompassing, leaving no thing or thought outside of the scope of Christ's redeeming love. This is a mystagogical masterpiece that carries more force than a Chuck Norris roundhouse-kick."

— Thomas V. Gourlay, Manager of Chaplaincy at
The University of Notre Dame Australia

"What are our lives about? The sacraments help us answer the questions of our existence and live as fully human beings. Fr. Harrison Ayre's *Mysterion* is a post-coronavirus gift for going deeper into the faith. Take and read, wherever you are on the journey of faith. Don't delay—jump in with the Trinity and Mary."

— Kathryn Jean Lopez, senior fellow,
National Review Institute

"The term 'sacramental worldview' has often been invoked in theology and catechesis alike in the twentieth century. Generally, it means a generic understanding of God's presence in the world. Fr. Ayre's *Mysterion* provides a correction to this approach to sacramentality. A sacramental worldview is necessarily ecclesial, bringing us into communion with Christ and each other in the Church. I cannot recommend this book enough for readers seeking to understand Catholicism."

— Timothy P. O'Malley, Ph.D., Director of Online
Education, McGrath Institute for Church Life;
Academic Director, Notre Dame Centre for Liturgy

MYS TER ION

MYS TER ION

The Revelatory Power
of the Sacramental Worldview

<small>FATHER HARRISON AYRE</small>

BOOKS & MEDIA

Boston

Nihil Obstat: Reverend Joseph Briody, S.S.L., S.T.D.

Imprimatur: ✠ Seán Cardinal O'Malley, O.F.M. Cap.
Archbishop of Boston
February 26, 2021

Library of Congress Control Number: 2021933124

CIP data is available.

ISBN 10: 0-8198-5016-0

ISBN 13: 978-0-8198-5016-4

Published by Pauline Books & Media, 50 Saint Pauls Avenue, Boston, MA 02130-3491

Printed in the U.S.A.

www.pauline.org

Pauline Books & Media is the publishing house of the Daughters of St. Paul, an international congregation of women religious serving the Church with the communications media.

1 2 3 4 5 6 7 8 9   26 25 24 23 22 21

To Mom and Dad,
thank you for everything.
I love you both more than you can know.

Contents

PART ONE

The Sacramental Worldview Explained

PART TWO

The Sacramental Worldview and the Church

PART THREE

Living the Sacramental Worldview

CHAPTER 7

CHAPTER 8

CHAPTER 9

Foreword

THE SACRAMENTAL WORLDVIEW, THOUGH LARGELY forgotten, is not an inaccessible, esoteric vision only scholars can comprehend. Thankfully, you do not need to be a theologian to read this book. Anyone who desires to live from and understand this worldview can do so. In fact, without being explicitly aware of it, some of the simplest, most faith-filled people already see the world through the sacramental worldview because they see it through the eyes of faith.

I was not introduced to the sacramental worldview in a class or a book but through my conversion from atheism. I had struggled for many years with the philosophical problem of the existence of the soul and, after much wrestling, came to the conclusion that the human soul did indeed exist. However, I could not make the intellectual step to believe in God's existence. Then, one day, as I was walking on a rural country road in Costa Rica, I was filled with gratitude for the beauty around me. At the same moment a sudden gust of wind tore through the trees and I feared that a tree might fall on me. I trembled at the realization of the precariousness of my being. It was in that moment that I realized that the fragile, beautiful, contingent being of the world, including my own self, had an absolute cause—a fearful, awesome cause—God.

In my conversion, I had what the French philosopher Jacques Maritain refers to as a "primordial intuition." The existence of the natural, material world led me to perceive a spiritual reality, the existence of God. Of course, knowledge of the existence of God is something that my human intelligence could have come to on its own, but I believe my intellect was aided by grace because God saw my struggle and resistance and had mercy on me. The multitudes of intelligent nonbelievers in the world show that what can be for some natural intuitions of God's existence do not come naturally to everyone. In fact, sometimes high intelligence can be an obstacle to intuiting the world's deepest realities. And on some level, we all struggle to comprehend and live according to the sacramental worldview in the modern world.

Truthful perceptions and intuitions of reality rely on a contemplative gaze, something that has become incredibly difficult to maintain in our hurried, noisy world. It's no coincidence that I became open to perceiving the existence of God through an experience in Costa Rica of slowing down, drinking in the beauty of nature, and dedicating myself to unhurried, patient manual labor. So many people are starved for these experiences in much of modern life. Additionally, many unwittingly live according to destructive modern ideologies and philosophies of the material world completely contrary to the sacramental worldview. As a result, many people reject Church teaching, especially in the areas of sexuality and ecclesiology, because they fail to understand the material world in the light of our faith.

Our modern way of living and thinking is so contrary to the sacramental worldview that apologetic arguments can only do so much in response to what is fundamentally a vision problem. For this reason, since my reversion to the faith, I have searched for effective ways to share the clarifying power of the sacramental worldview because I know how life-changing it can be. But I have struggled to find the words to explain something that came to me in a flash of grace. I have searched for a book on a popular level that explains the sacramental vision, but it's a sorely neglected topic in the Church. Many books have been written on the Mass and the seven sacraments, but few delve more deeply into the fundamental structure of the universe, which informs these basic aspects of our faith. Why? Based on my experience in ministry, I would venture to guess that, unfortunately, few people explicitly think about the faith in these terms.

I am delighted and honored to have worked with Father Harrison Ayre in the process of bringing this book to life. For so long, I have wanted to find a clear explanation of the revelatory power of the Catholic worldview to share with people. I am confident that his book will help many people to remove the blindfolds of tainted, injurious worldviews and put on the clear, defining prescription glasses of our faith. I pray that a deeper understanding of the sacramental worldview will change your life as it has changed mine, and that it enable you to participate more in Christ who lives and dwells within us through our Baptism.

Sr. Theresa Aletheia Noble, FSP

Preface

THIS BOOK IS MY ATTEMPT to bring together the different topics I've spoken about on my podcast *Clerically Speaking*, in my research and studies, and as the fruit of my prayer and pastoral experience. I will caution that this book attempts to enlighten rather than to offer practical tips. This is not to say that practical matters aren't important, but the Christian tradition—especially the Church's sacramental vision—begins in contemplation and prayer. By being enlightened through this life of prayer, we start to see life differently and to live it differently in practice. So much of what is written in this book doesn't only come from theological studies; it comes from pastoral experience as well. I am very keen on the idea that theology has to be rooted in both prayer and pastoral work. This book is meant to challenge some preconceptions we have about Christian living and encourage us in areas of weakness so that, both through reading this book and living our Christian life, we can attain a deeper communion with Christ and his Church.

A small grace occurred while I was writing this book. When I submitted my writing sample to Sr. Theresa, she told me after the book was accepted that much of what I had to say was very Pauline. Over the years I've been attracted more and more to the Pauline charism. The Pauline charism encompasses the mission of evangelizing through the modern means of communication and is also deeply bound up in the theology of the letters of Saint Paul. The Pauline charism and spirituality are centered on the person of Jesus as the Way, the Truth, and the Life, inviting each of us to learn from Jesus and allowing the Holy Spirit to form Jesus *in* us. As I was writing this book, I was reading some of the writings of Blessed James Alberione, founder of the Pauline Family. I found in him a kindred spirit and an advocate for what I want to propose in this book: that to be a Christian means to really live and participate in the life of Christ. Blessed Alberione was inspired by the writings of Saint Paul, who teaches us that Christ is to be formed in each and every person. What is proposed in this book, then, is not some innovation, but is rooted deeply in the tradition and in the teachings of Saint Paul himself. I've come to recognize that the Pauline community sees how important the idea of participation is to the Christian life and how central it is to the teaching of the New Testament. Thanks to writing this book, I am eager to get to know Blessed Alberione all the more. I encourage you to discover his writings as well.

This book is an attempt to express the idea that the word "sacrament" has a broader and deeper meaning than we often give it. We are going to explore the idea that we always have access to the life of Christ *today*, principally through the Church and the life of discipleship, but also by looking to the whole of creation and seeing it as a sign that points us to God.

This book is meant, then, not so much to propose new tools and new habits of living, but to propose a new and deeper vision of reality based in the heart of the Church's tradition and teaching. This vision is none other than to share in Christ's own vision of creation, to share in his life, and to allow his life to live in us: the sacramental vision is meant to help us see that always and everywhere, in a mysterious way, we are participating in the life of Christ.

Acknowledgments

A BOOK, I HAVE DISCOVERED, is not a solo project, especially when it's someone's first writing project. I must always begin by thanking my family, who helped nurture me to become the man I am today, especially my parents, Lindsay and Estelle. During the process of writing, they constantly cheered me on and encouraged me toward the goal of finishing this book.

A big thank you to Sr. Theresa Aletheia, Noble, FSP. It was she who coaxed me into this adventure in the first place, helped me along as I began, cheered me on through the writing process, was an ear who would listen, and gave me great encouragement and advice going forward. I would often text her through the ups and downs, when new insights would hit, and she would patiently respond with an encouraging word. Her friendship and assistance in all this have made this book possible. I also had the privilege of working with Courtney Saponaro in this process. Her fresh look at the manuscript, her flexibility, and her helpful comments helped this book grow to be what it is.

My dear friends Shannon and Jonathan Last have also contributed much. Right when all this was starting, Jonathan gave me some helpful writing tips that I've been slowly, though imperfectly, attempting to internalize and implement. Shannon was my second pair of eyes throughout the writing process. Not only did she help me refine my style, but she would tell me if I was being too academic, or if something simply wasn't clear. She edited and was a friend I could bounce ideas off of, or simply ask for tips in the writing process. The friendship of both Jonathan and Shannon has proven invaluable.

A massive thank you to my *Clerically Speaking* co-host Father Anthony Sciarappa, who over the course of these last couple of years has had to put up with my intellectual rabbit holes. Many of the ideas in this book are the result of different podcast episodes that helped me see the central theme presented here. I am especially grateful to my theological mentor, Father Don MacDonald, OFM. I cherish the memories of the many theological discussions we had when I would visit him at the friary during my years in seminary, and his help especially as the advisor for my master's thesis. It is no understatement to say that a large chunk of this book is due to his influence and I'm immensely grateful for his friendship and mentorship over the years.

Thank you to Bishop Gary Gordon, who has been supportive of both my writing and intellectual endeavors as I've served as one of his priests in the diocese of Victoria. I also owe much of this book to Father John Laszczyk, without whom I would not be a priest today, and whose mentorship over the years has brought me to this point.

I want to thank Rachel and Jason Bulman, Peter Gubbels, Michael Heinlein, Timothy Troutner, Chris McCaffe, Hogan Herritage, Father Matt Fish, Father David Hogman, and anyone else with whom I've conversed about the various themes of this book. As all my friends know, I am an external processor and I need to talk things out, so I'm grateful for their patience and help when working out many of these ideas over the past years.

Finally, a word of thanks must always be given to God. It is God who inspires, strengthens, and guides. I've spent countless hours in prayer over what I've been writing, and God has often given me an inspiration—whether through Scripture, spiritual reading, or an idea suddenly popping into my head. He has shown his tender care and mercy to me along the way and continues to guide me. All of this is to his glory, so that it can hopefully help, in some small fashion, to bring about the glory of his kingdom. All praise and glory be to God the Father, Son, and Holy Spirit.

Introduction

WE ARE ALWAYS AND EVERYWHERE "in Christ." Reflect on that statement for a minute, ponder the meaning of the word "in," think of it in all its literalness: that is what our life is like as Christians. We are in the life of Christ, and he lives his life in us. In everything we do as Christians—from our prayer life to attempts to practice virtue and avoid sin—we are acting *in Christ*, and thereby, through his grace, becoming the saints he calls us to be.

To be a Christian means to really participate in the life of Christ and allow Christ and the mysteries of his life, death, and resurrection to work in us. But what do we mean by "mystery"? In Ephesians 5:32, Saint Paul writes, "This is a great mystery . . . I speak in reference to Christ and the church." The word Paul uses for "mystery" is the Greek word *mysterion*. In a modern context, when we hear the word "mystery," we often think of something that needs to be solved and completed, like a murder mystery or a crossword puzzle. When we don't know how something is going to unfold, there's mystery involved, a sense of the unknown. But eventually we come to some sort of resolution, and there's no longer any mystery. However, Saint Paul and the other earliest Christian writers, commonly called the Church Fathers, did not use the word "mystery" in the same way.

When Saint Paul writes that the Church or Christ is a "mystery," he is not only referring to a sense of hiddenness or concealment. If this were the case, Christianity would fall into irrationality, for it would only deal with what is invisible. We as human beings come to knowledge through the senses of taste, touch, smell, hearing, and sight. If we could never come to know about the faith in this way, then the whole of Christianity would be undermined. The mystery of God is *revealed* in the incarnation of Jesus. God *shows* himself to us through the human nature of Jesus Christ.

In other words, through the revelation in Christ's Incarnation, God makes known what is hidden: he makes it visible in Christ. The fact that the mystery of God is revealed in the Person of Jesus Christ tells us that at the heart of the concept of mystery is the Son of God, Jesus Christ. Christ "has made known to us the mystery of his will" (Eph 1:9). In fact, Saint Paul calls Christ "the mystery of God" (Col 2:2). Jesus makes visible what is invisible in God. We could sum up the word "mystery" by simply saying: in the Christian tradition, mystery refers to something visible that was previously invisible, the pinnacle of which is Jesus Christ. But how is "mystery" related to "sacrament"? More closely than one might think.

The Greek word "mysterion" is translated into Latin as *sacramentum* or "sacrament." If we look at the basic definition of sacrament from the *Catechism of the Catholic Church*, we can begin to understand the connection between mystery and sacrament. A sacrament is "the visible sign of the hidden reality of salvation."[1] A sacrament makes present and active something we cannot see directly. These invisible realities that the sacraments make present are nothing other than the works of Christ. Why does God work this way with the sacraments? It's quite simple: our knowledge comes from our senses. We can only know something if we see, hear, taste, touch, or smell it. Since God created us to know through our senses, he uses them to communicate his life to us: through our senses, we come to know who God is.

Sacramentality is not simply a way God communicates himself to us in the Church; it is rooted in how he has structured all of creation. For example, on a fundamental level, the body makes our personhood visible and present to others: we are embodied persons who make ourselves present to others through our bodies. Words, too, are themselves a sacrament: the sound waves of our voice vibrating through the air into the ear drums of another communicate an idea we want to express. The physical—the voice—makes present the invisible—the idea or concept we want to communicate. If this is how creation is structured, then would God not build the Church upon this natural sacramental foundation? Hence, the Church also sees herself as a sacrament. *Lumen Gentium*, a document on the Church from the Second Vatican Council,

---

1. *Catechism of the Catholic Church* (United States Catholic Conference, Inc., Libreria Editrice Vaticana, 1994), no. 774.

calls the Church the "universal sacrament of salvation."[2] By this, the council means to communicate that the Church really makes Jesus' salvation visible to the world. Therefore, every baptized person shares in the Church's mission to make Christ's saving mystery known and present to everyone.

We see quite quickly, based on the above, that sacramentality is at the heart of the Christian life because it's structured into our very existence. God communicates to us in this fashion, and makes himself present in this fashion, because this is how we know and experience life: it's how he has created us. But sacramentality is not just about seeing God through his creation; it also means "participation": God uses the material world to draw us into his very life. Saint Paul speaks of this idea of participation in one of the most consequential phrases of the New Testament: we are "in Christ." To be "in Christ" is to live in him with his life living in us. To live as a Christian is to understand that we are "in Christ" more than we are in our house, our office building, our car, or anywhere else. For the Christian, Baptism establishes a real communion between us and God whereby he is always actively living his life in us.

The sacramental worldview, then, means seeing everything created and physical as pointing us to God and lifting us into his life. As the psalmist writes, "The heavens declare

---

2. Second Vatican Ecumenical Council, *Lumen Gentium*, no. 48, https://www.vatican.va/archive/hist_councils/ii_vatican_council/documents/vat-ii_const_19641121 _lumen-gentium_en.html.

the glory of God" (Ps 19:2). In other words, God's creation both points to and participates in God's glory, in his very life. Saint Paul also points to the centrality of this view in his Letter to the Romans: "What can be known about God is evident to them, because God made it evident to them. Ever since the creation of the world, his invisible attributes of eternal power and divinity have been able to be understood and perceived in what he has made" (1:19–20). Everything created points us toward God because the physical can make us aware of the invisible and even make it present, thereby allowing us to participate in God's life.

God's presence in the world and in the Christian life is always active, drawing us deeper into the mystery of Christ. This means that our lives are always being touched by the mystery of Jesus' life, death, and resurrection. Everything either points us toward greater communion or tends to draw us away from God toward sin. The goal of this book is to draw you in the right direction—into relationship with Jesus. A real, personal, and living relationship with Jesus. But a personal relationship always occurs through Jesus' body, the Church, and is built up through the reading of Scripture, the life of the sacraments, and interactions with other members of Christ's body. In other words, a personal relationship with Jesus is always rooted in the communion of the Church and built up *through* the Church.

The goal of this book is to help you see that this life in Christ is alive and active in all aspects of Christian living. The sacramental worldview, as it's proposed in this book, helps us to see that Christ is always drawing us really and truly to the Father. Thus, this book's ultimate goal is to help you grow in your life with Christ. The book is structured around the central theses we are going to explore in Chapters 1 and 2, where we will discover just how the Church understands the word sacrament and how the concept is broader, deeper, and more active than you may have known. We want to move away from a reductive sense of seeing sacramentality as just the seven sacraments—as important as they are!—toward an understanding that sacrament is really one of the key themes of the Christian life. The themes brought out in Chapter 1 are furthered in Chapter 2 by looking at what it means to be "in Christ." The fact is, we are always "in Christ" by virtue of our Baptism. This fact opens up for us avenues of seeing God as really and truly living in us: our whole life is "in Christ."

Yet, despite hearing about all the wonderful truths of sacramentality, we often struggle to see it as something we can really embrace as a way to live. Chapter 3 will address some of our obstacles by discussing the heresy of modernism. That chapter attempts to provide a balanced understanding of what modernism is and how it has created an obstacle to seeing the world sacramentally; it will briefly present a sort of apologetics or argument against modernism to help create a rational basis for the sacramental vision. The fact is, we are inundated with a worldview that undermines our ability to see how we live in Christ. By clearing away the brush of modernism, we will have smoother footing for moving forward.

To really embrace a sacramental vision of the Christian faith, we cannot ignore the Church. As we will come to see, faith is given to us through the Church, and it is precisely faith that makes us able to see God through the stuff of this world and to participate in the life of the Trinity. Chapters 4 and 5 will explore the nature of the Church, its centrality and importance. This will help us discover how the Church herself is a sacrament. This is central to moving forward, because so often aspects of the Church—her structures and rituals—are seen as obstacles to faith when, in fact, they are the very means by which we come to faith.

Our journey into sacramentality will take a brief excursus in Chapter 6 by looking at the figure of Mary. Mary is the archetype—the perfect image—of the Church. In Mary, we see what Christ's Church ought to look like and, moreover, we see how we ought to approach Christian living. In Mary we discover the attitudes that are essential for building up our sacramental vision. We will, therefore, look to her so as to see Christ as she sees him and thus begin to cultivate the attitude of heart necessary for embracing the sacramental and participatory worldview.

These chapters lead us to the final part of the book where, having considered what the sacramental worldview is, and why the Church is essential to it, we can discover how the sacramental worldview is lived. Chapters 7 and 8 will explore liturgy on a broader level and look more particularly at the Mass to see, in a cursory fashion, how the Church's whole liturgical life is one of the central places where we encounter God and are lifted up into his life.

But the Christian life is not solely liturgical, as important as liturgy is. Christian life is also rooted in prayer and discipleship. Chapter 9 is going to help us see that personal prayer is a privileged place where we encounter and are lifted up into Christ's life. The life of prayer is one of the hidden jewels of the Catholic faith, so Chapter 9 will offer some examples of prayer and how they help us participate in the life of Christ.

Chapter 10 will look at how our life as Christians, in actions, sufferings, and our pursuit of virtue, is itself a living out in us of the mystery of Christ's death and resurrection. In other words, Christian discipleship is a daily living out in our lives of the mystery of Christ's love for us and for the world.

I have always been struck by the principle that one of my favorite theologians lived by: "theology is always done on one's knees." This is a principle that Hans Urs von Balthasar believed and promoted through his theological work. What he means by this phrase is that holiness and theology are not opposed to each other, but rather depend on each other. We must dwell upon our encounters with the Lord and allow what we study to impact and imbue our life of prayer and discipleship. Really, Balthasar's principle can be called the soul of this book: it's the uniting principle around the endeavor we are about to embark on together. The life of the Christian is not bifurcated into separate compartments, but rather, sees the whole as encompassing the mind, heart, and soul. In many ways, the unity of theology and spirituality—of truth and holiness—is immersed in the sacramental world-view. When we are pursuing truth, we are not pursuing an idea, but rather a Person, Jesus Christ. We participate in Christ: his life in ours, our life in his. Everything that constitutes our being human, not just our soul, but our mind too, participates in his life and helps us draw close to him. Thus, the truth we discover is nothing more than the Christ in whose life we live. My hope is that the theology you encounter in this book will enrich your spiritual life, and that the spiritual principles we explore will be reflected on and pondered, so that Christ can be all in all in you.

PART ONE

The Sacramental Worldview Explained

CHAPTER 1

Mystery and Sacrament

NO TRIP TO SPAIN IS complete without a visit to Barcelona to see the basilica designed by Antoni Gaudi, the *Sagrada Familia*. Though consecrated by Pope Benedict XVI in 2010 and hailed as a shining example of what modern Christian architecture can accomplish, Gaudi's masterpiece remains unfinished. Despite its being perpetually under construction, thousands of tourists and pilgrims visit daily, drawn by its beauty. As one enters the basilica through the Holy Family façade, it's impossible not to feel awe and reverence. Both traditional yet intensely earthly, the façade seems to be almost rising straight out of mud. The pillars are like giant tree trunks in a rainforest, supporting the immense, colorful ceiling. All of Gaudi's architecture is similarly imbued with a strong naturalism that reflects the belief that the created world is inherently good. His major architectural insight was that nature has no straight lines. If this is the case with nature, he reasoned, why does architecture depend upon straight lines? Yet at the same time Gaudi was also a man of tradition, embracing classical Gothic design, seen particularly in the basilica's majestic steeples that point the eye toward heaven. From the more earthy tones of the lower levels of the basilica to the celestial feeling of the upper portions, the structure moves the eye from the realm of the physical and natural to the realm of the spiritual and supernatural. The *Sagrada Familia* is a testament to beauty, and like all beauty, it leaves us in a state of wonder.

Ponder, for a moment, a time you experienced something truly beautiful. Think of the feelings that washed over you, the indescribable joy you felt in every pore. Remember how distractions ceased. Perhaps you simply wanted time to stop so you could gaze forever at this beautiful object. Beauty is not something simply external to us. It captures all our senses. It enraptures us, captivates us, draws us into its very life, and points us to the deeper meanings it attempts to convey.

True beauty gives meaning to a core observation of philosophy: the whole is greater than the sum of its parts. This is difficult for us to see because we are overwhelmed by the worldview of scientism. Scientism is very much a fruit of the Enlightenment, and at its heart it wants to see the world only according to its mechanics—how it works and functions. It says that the only real knowledge, the only real way to interpret and see the world, is through the scientific method. Scientism proposes life without beauty. It measures, dissects, gauges, and analyzes without appreciating the object itself. Presented with a flower, scientism would note its color and how it achieves said color, measure the stem, and expound on the mechanics of floral biology. Scientism can only see the parts; it can never see the whole.

In no way does this mean that science is unnecessary or bad. Science has its rightful place within the Catholic worldview, which values both faith and reason. Scientism, however, only examines the world scientifically without appreciating other, fuller, more essential ways of seeing and experiencing it. Beauty, therefore, cannot be measured by science. We may note the perfect coloring of a particular flower, but this observation merely helps us appreciate the totality of the flower's beauty. This truth aligns with the way we naturally speak about things. How dull life would be if our conversations involved, for instance, the mechanisms of floral biology rather than exuberant descriptions of the exquisite flowers we saw during a walk through a field!

Experiencing beauty involves perceiving the parts in concert with the whole, and this helps us perceive things that lie beyond our senses. When we allow ourselves to be arrested in front of something beautiful, we allow ourselves to experience something mysterious. We can't observe beauty quickly and move on. We need to contemplate it, allow it to seep into us so that we can understand, know, and appreciate it in countless indescribable ways. Imperceptibly, beauty changes us. Behind every appreciation of beauty is an experience of mystery, and mystery is the vehicle by which beauty is manifested. "How is this related to the sacramental worldview?" you might ask. Beauty is at the heart of the sacramental worldview because it draws us to perceive our participation in the life of Christ in a deeper way.

Beauty draws us to see the "something more" of the world. The sacramental worldview is, at its heart, the recognition of the power of the beautiful to open us up to God's grace. When we encounter beauty, either in nature or in the life of the Church, the experience of seeing the whole also draws out of us a profound experience of mystery and awe. Think of anything beautiful you've seen, anything truly breathtaking: don't we often experience awe and wonder in those moments? Think about the joy that comes in these moments. All of this leaves us with an ability to see that there is "something more." Wonder, awe, joy: these reactions of ours to the beautiful help us understand that there is a "something more" to all things, something we can see but not grasp. At the heart of beauty, then, is mystery, because what is mystery but an awe toward the "something more"?

Mystery

As we discussed in the introduction, the word *mystery* can have all sorts of associations for us. Often the phrase "it's a mystery" is used to mean that the answer is unknown. When it comes to faith, probably all of us have heard the word *mystery* used dismissively: "Oh, the Trinity is a mystery, I can't bother to try to understand it." While it's true that the Trinity is a mystery, the mysterious aspect of God can be used as an excuse to repress inquisitiveness and attempts to understand. Perhaps we do this when we see the mystery as too insurmountable, too difficult to attempt to penetrate.

However, the Christian notion of mystery is vastly different. In this chapter we will discuss its rich tradition and precise meaning in the Scriptures. Mystery can be categorized into four essential elements:

1) concealment;

2) revelation of God's saving activity;

3) ritual participation in God's saving deeds, and

4) connection to *sacrament*.

Mystery as Concealment

The word "concealment" finds its roots in two Latin words: *con*, which means "with," and *celare*, which means "to hide." To conceal, then, is "to hide with." Veiled and hidden, the mystery of God exists in the heart of God alone: "Oh, the depth of the riches of the wisdom and knowledge of God! How inscrutable are his judgments and how unsearchable his ways! 'For who has known the mind of the Lord or who has been his counselor?'" (Rom 11:33–34). These words from Saint Paul present a longstanding biblical truth: the human mind cannot grasp the mind of God. The depths of God are concealed from us and cannot be exhausted, nor can we force God to be known according to our terms. Therefore, we must respect God's transcendence, or, to put it differently, God's otherness.

But why is it necessary for God to conceal himself and his plans? Why must God put a veil between himself and his creation? It's normal to sometimes find God's concealment frustrating. It can even tempt us to doubt his existence. This doubt is partially due to how we see the world: often we are unable to let the world point to something beyond what's before our eyes. Yet, this is a legitimate question: if God is who he says he is, why can't he show himself more clearly?

Often such a question leaves out a central aspect of our humanity that affects every moment of our lives—we are creatures born into a fallen world. The Fall had an impact not just on us individually, but on all creation. Adam and Eve were created to offer all of creation back to God. Instead, they took creation into their own hands. Consequently, we live in a creation that rebels against God. Our fallen nature finds its roots in the taking of the fruit of the tree of the knowledge of good and evil, in attempting to become like God on our own terms. Because our first parents didn't offer creation back to God, taking the fruit was their way of alienating creation from God. Thus, all of creation became affected by the sin of our first parents. All of creation is now oriented away from God.

At this point, it's important to note that God still loves us, but *he does not love sin.* For this reason, he changed how he related to the world—not for his sake, but for our sake, so that we would return to him with true self-giving love instead of selfishly attempting to manipulate him for our own ends and goals. God mysteriously hid himself so as to bring us and all of creation back into right order.

Let's face an uncomfortable truth: If God dwelt with us now in the way he did prior to the Fall, we, too, would try to bring him down to our own level. We, too, would attempt to manipulate and use him to achieve our own goals. We, too, would make an idol out of God! This is the heart of idolatry: it's not only an attempt to worship false gods, but also an attempt to worship God falsely. Once we begin to understand that we are fallen creatures who need to reorient our lives and all of creation in the direction of self-giving love, then it becomes clearer why God is concealed from us. He is concealed so that we will not use him wrongly, so that he can begin to draw us into the life of love.

Yet, this concealment isn't only for God's sake, but for our sake as well. Parents do not tell their two-year-old all the moral and life lessons the toddler will need to know later; rather, as the child grows older, the parents slowly teach more lessons to him or her, helping the young person grow into greater maturity. It's the same with God. God does not reveal his whole plan and purpose for us immediately. But throughout salvation history, slowly, with the patience of a loving parent, he reveals his plans and purposes to us until we come to full maturity when he sends his Son into the world. Throughout the whole Old Testament, God increasingly reveals his nature and mercy to Israel. To Abraham, Moses, David, and the prophets he slowly reveals his heart so as to prepare Israel and all humanity for his final revelation: his Son. God reveals these plans to us in a very particular way: his plans, his desires for us, are always revealed through his saving actions.

Mystery as a Saving Activity

In the Old Testament, from the moment of the Fall, God tells us that plans are in motion to bring about our redemption. He promises a victory over the serpent, that is, the devil (see Gn 3:14–15). God's plans continue with Noah, through whom he saves the human race with a small and faithful remnant. After the flood, God chooses Abraham, through whom he establishes Israel. These saving plans continue as God rescues the Israelites from Egypt and guides them through a time of purification in the desert, then places Israel in its chosen land, and eventually establishes a kingdom in David. When Israel goes astray, God allows the Israelites to be purified through suffering and exile so they can be drawn back to their mission of being a light to the nations. Then God sends prophets within Israel to help the people to remember Israel's mission. These prophets also foreshadow a time when God will act in a definitive manner. Through symbols, images, and prophetic words, God enacts the foretelling of the coming of a new Moses, who will finally save his people Israel.

God does not reveal his plan all at once. In all of this, God reveals himself only through saving actions: every action is tied to a salvation and thereby reveals to us something of who God is. Sometimes this involves revealing in a more direct manner, as with Noah, Abraham, and the Israelites in their escape from Egypt; other times, in a more indirect fashion, as through the invasion of Babylon or the words of the prophets. Regardless of the form that God's intervention takes, an overarching theme emerges as, slowly, God begins to unveil himself and his plans. This is why the entire Old Testament is so important to Christians. As the Letter to the Hebrews says, "In times past, God spoke in partial and various ways to our ancestors through the prophets; in these last days, he spoke to us through a son, whom he made heir of all things and through whom he created the universe" (1:1–2). The entirety of God's plan points in a hidden way to the definitive revelation that happens in Jesus Christ.

In fact, Saint Paul refers to Jesus a few times as the "mystery of God" (see Col 1:27; 2:2; 4:3). For Paul, this mystery of God—the activity of God in the past—now comes unexpectedly to fulfillment in the saving activity of Jesus Christ.

Thus *mystery*, in Paul's use of the term, implies both a saving action and a revelation. God reveals himself to us *through* his saving actions, and the most perfect saving action is the cross and resurrection where God is revealed as the Trinity. It is on the cross that the Son, by the power of the Holy Spirit, offers himself to the Father and in the resurrection that the Father raises the Son from the dead by the Holy Spirit. The paschal mystery, then, reveals who God is: Father, Son, and Holy Spirit. Thus, Jesus is not only the Savior of the world; he is also the revealer of God to us: "Whoever has seen me has seen the Father" (Jn 14:9). Mystery, then, is God saving us and at the same time revealing who he is.

Mystery as Participation

Now, you might be thinking, "This is all well and good, but Jesus saved us two thousand years ago and I can't go back in time. How can these saving and revealing mysteries of God be accessible to me today?" This brings us to the third aspect of mystery: participation. As we've discussed, God's plans are hidden in himself. But he reveals them through his saving actions. And these saving actions aren't fossilized in history; they are alive and accessible to us today through liturgy, through the Mass. Every time we go to Mass anywhere in the world, the priest proclaims these words after the consecration of the Eucharist: "The mystery of faith." Basically, he's saying, "The secrets of God's heart, that are made known to us and save us in Jesus Christ, have been sacramentally represented on the altar." By proclaiming this to the faithful at Mass, the priest reminds everyone that God is here, that he is saving his people, and that he is showing himself—not only two thousand years ago but now.

Moreover, God asks us to participate in his plans right now. He's not asking us to participate in a sort of activism, whereby liturgy becomes merely an expression of community togetherness. He's declaring that the Church is present in a particular place and time—this time!—and that we, the Church, are being drawn into the universal saving and revealing mystery of Jesus' cross and resurrection. Liturgy, instituted by Christ and developed by the Church, is a ritualized way for us to access his salvation. We will unpack this amazing mystery more later in Chapter 7 when we talk about the liturgical life.

Mystery as Sacrament

This brings us to the fourth and final understanding of mystery. When Saint Jerome was translating the Bible into Latin in the fourth and fifth centuries, he used a peculiar word to translate the Greek word for mystery—*mysterion*—into Latin. He chose the word *sacramentum,* or sacrament. For example, in his Letter to the Ephesians, Paul describes how marriage images Christ's love for the Church: "This is a great mystery, but I speak in reference to Christ and the Church" (5:32). Where Paul uses the word *mysterion*, Jerome translates it as *sacramentum.* In other words, the great nuptial analogy Paul has just used to describe the meaning of Christ's relationship with the Church means that marriage is a *sacrament* of this relationship. Marriage on earth is something visible that makes present and efficacious something that is invisible.

What's invisible? The relationship between Christ and his Church. What's visible? The marital love between husband and wife. The Christ-centered love of husband for wife and wife for husband is meant to be a sign that makes visible the invisible and spiritual reality of Christ's love for his Church.

This fourth sense of the word *mystery*, then, brings together everything we have said thus far. Sacramentality, as we are going to discover, moves beyond just the seven sacraments. It means that God is using everything in his Church and in creation to bring about the redemption of humanity. God communicates himself, his plans, his saving actions *through* creation. God holds his plans in secret, in his heart, from all eternity, but he slowly unveils them in history in various times and places. God's plans and revelation culminate in the ultimate saving and revealing action of Jesus in the paschal mystery. This action of God is now something we all have a chance to be present at and to participate in through the liturgical and sacramental life of the Church. God makes his actions present and effective to us through tangible signs—sacraments—and allows us to receive our salvation. And we can only receive salvation by participation in Christ, the ultimate mystery of God made flesh.

CHAPTER 2

Participation in Christ

IN THE GOSPEL OF JOHN, Jesus says to his disciples, "I am the Way and the Truth and the Life. No one comes to the Father except through me" (14:6). Here we see something utterly unique compared to other world religions. While many religious figures present themselves as teachers about wisdom and salvation, they do not present themselves as the means to salvation. Jesus makes himself the center of his message: only in him can we have eternal life. This is why Jesus does not call himself a way, a truth, or a life; he uses the definite article "the." To put it differently, Jesus does not present himself as just one option of salvation among many. The path to God is not a spiritual buffet where we pick and choose whichever way we prefer according to what seems to suit us best. No. Jesus declares himself to be *the* Way, *the* Truth, *the* Life. To choose Jesus is to choose *the* path to God. Because Jesus is the mystery of God, he makes visible God's hidden plans. Jesus is the definitive way to God because, by his saving actions on the cross and in the resurrection, he reveals the heart of God.

Following this provocative statement from Jesus, we hear the second claim: "no one comes to the Father except through me." Making the choice to follow Jesus is one part of the Christian life, but the preposition "through" is what the choice implies. The choice for Jesus' way is not only exemplary—we do not merely imitate him. Rather, we really enter into his life. This phrase may not hit home with the depth it implies; it may roll off the page and into our mind rather passively. But when Jesus says that to come to the Father we must go *through him*, he is saying we must really allow his life to live in us and allow ourselves to live in him.

"In Christ"

To choose Jesus means to live "in Christ." These two simple words are repeated around eighty times in Scripture, mostly in Saint Paul's epistles. This phrase proclaims that our life is a participation in Jesus' life, death, and resurrection. To put it differently, to live *in Christ* proposes that we live *sacramentally*. It means that my whole life—body, mind, soul, intellect, will, the whole of my person—is conformed to Christ, is brought into union with him through Baptism, and is thereby given a mysterious participation in the events of his life. All that Jesus spoke, did, and accomplished in his life is now lived out in his body, the Church. This is the sacramental vision of Christianity.

Remember: a sacrament makes present and visible something invisible. Because of our Baptism, the mysteries of

Christ's life are always made present to us. They are lived out in the Church and, through her, in us individually. For this reason Saint Paul exclaims that we are "always carrying about in the body the dying of Jesus, so that the life of Jesus may also be manifested in our body" (2 Cor 4:10). Because of Baptism, we make Christ's death and resurrection visible through us. Not only that, through our participation in Christ's death and resurrection in Baptism, we are always vehicles of Christ's presence and, therefore, his grace to the whole world. The whole world is to see Christ sacramentally present in us.

In case this concept isn't clear, Saint Paul emphasizes it over and over again in his epistles. For instance, in his Letter to the Romans he writes:

> Or are you unaware that we who were baptized into Christ Jesus were baptized into his death? We were indeed buried with him through baptism into death, so that, just as Christ was raised from the dead by the glory of the Father, we too might live in newness of life.
>
> For if we have grown into union with him through a death like his, we shall also be united with him in the resurrection. We know that our old self was crucified with him, so that our sinful body might be done away with, that we might no longer be in slavery to sin. For a dead person has been absolved from sin. If, then, we have died with Christ, we believe that we shall also live with him. We know that Christ, raised from the dead, dies no more; death no longer has power over him. As to his death, he died to sin once and for all; as to his life, he lives for God. Consequently, you too must think of yourselves as [being] dead to sin and living for God in Christ Jesus.

Romans 6:3–11

What Paul is saying here is simply that through Baptism we are immersed into the death and resurrection of Jesus. Baptism makes us sharers of his very life. When Christ died, we, through Baptism, died with him. When Christ was raised from the dead, we, through Baptism, were raised with him. So now we are alive in Christ Jesus: our life is now "hidden with Christ in God" (Col 3:3).

In order for us to understand the life of Christ being lived in us through Baptism, we need to briefly reflect on an even more fundamental truth of our faith and the real heart of the sacramental vision: the Incarnation. In the Incarnation, the Son of God became man in Jesus Christ. He took our humanity upon himself, thereby uniting himself not only with all humanity, but, in a way, with all creation as well. This amazing act of God is an affirmation of the soul, the body, and indeed all the material world. But what is even more amazing is that God's affirmation doesn't end with a simple taking of our nature, but because Jesus is at the right hand of the Father as the first fruits of our redemption, it is a sign that all of creation is to dwell with God. This is important because it shows that the spiritual and the material are not opposed or in competition, but rather exist in communion with each other. In the Incarnation, Jesus' divinity never overwhelms his humanity, and his humanity never limits his divinity. Rather, their communion is a sign of how God relates to all of the created order in its spiritual and material domains. The Incarnation demonstrates that the material world really can be used by God.

Thus, by virtue of the Incarnation, God has touched all of humanity in Christ. He is the new Adam, the new blueprint of humanity. Therefore, we no longer find our identity in the fallen Adam, but in the resurrected Christ. We've moved from participating in the fall of Adam to participating in the saving mysteries of Jesus' life, death, and resurrection. Baptism unites us to this restored humanity, and our life is now really and truly "in Christ" because Christ is "in us" through the Incarnation and Baptism.

The Meeting of Time and Eternity

One of the most amazing implications of the Incarnation is that in Jesus Christ time and eternity come together. By taking on our human nature, Jesus has taken on not only our body, but everything associated with being human. Part of what he takes, then, is humanity's experience of time, and he brings it into eternity. This may be difficult to comprehend at first, but bear with me. If God, who exists outside of time, took on our humanity, he also took on our linear experience of time. We experience time, generally, as something that moves from one moment to the next. Once a moment passes, it can never return except through our memory. We can't travel back or forth in time. Time comes, and time goes. This was the experience of time that Jesus had in his humanity. Because Jesus is fully God and fully man, the union that happens in his Person is not just that of two natures, but of time and eternity as well—something amazing that has profound implications for a sacramental worldview.

In Jesus Christ, eternity is made present to us through his humanity in time and space, and time and space are lifted up into God's eternity! Why is this so important? Because it means that the words, actions, and saving acts of Jesus that happened two thousand years ago in Jerusalem are not just events of the past. Because of this union of time and eternity, these events are now always present. This is why the Book of Revelation speaks of the Lamb "standing as though slain" (see Rev 5:6). It's a symbolic way of speaking about Jesus crucified and risen at the same time. We can do that because these two separate events in time—the death of Jesus and his victorious resurrection—are now both eternally present. Eternity makes whatever is in it always and everywhere present. In other words, it's always "now" in God.

Thus, the events of Jesus' life are now eternally available to the Christian through the life of the Church. The liturgical calendar, for example, lays out different points of the year where the Church wants to emphasize and access particular actions of Jesus' saving ministry. In this way, Jesus is not distant or far away, but always and everywhere applying the fruits of his paschal mystery to a world in need of salvation. And this always happens through the liturgical, sacramental, and spiritual life of the Church—the means by which we have access to these saving realities. The liturgy is the means by which we participate in Christ's saving actions today.

All of this is understood through a particular word that was used in the early Church: *recapitulation.* In its most literal sense, the word means placing everything under the headship of one person, bringing things back into unity under a singular head. Because Christ has become man, because he has entered the mysteries of sin and death, he has now established a Church which is "his body, the fullness of the one who fills all things in every way" (Eph 1:23). In other words, Jesus is now present through the Church to always make his paschal mystery present, to make the fullness of his life present to all the faithful throughout all of time. All of history finds its completion and culmination in Jesus because now all time belongs to him. Because he is now universally present to all time through his Church, he is constantly endowing creation with his salvation so that it can share in this fullness of life.

Without this concept of time and eternity coming together in Jesus Christ, the sacramental vision would be an impossibility. For example, Jesus would only be a character of the past, not someone alive and active today, mysteriously drawing the world into his eternity. The Scriptures would be mere books telling of past events. The importance, then, of time and eternity coming together in Jesus Christ means that the past not only comes alive today, but that it's alive so we can participate in the mysteries of Jesus' salvation, and thereby be saved.

What Is the Sacramental Worldview?

In these past two chapters, we have given a theological underpinning to the sacramental worldview. This act of theologizing is important because God gave us the gifts of our minds to reflect and know more deeply the mystery of his love. Thus, we've really become theologians in these first couple of chapters: we've reflected on the mystery of faith and have come to know this mystery more fully through thought, reflection, and prayer. All of what we have done so far now becomes the framework around which we can begin to understand and delve into the sacramental vision. The sacramental vision is nothing other than this: to participate in the life of Christ. By being "in Christ," we now see the world through his eyes, and can see that our whole life is a means of encounter with him. Let's break this down by recapping everything we've talked about so far.

First, the sacramental worldview recognizes that God always works through his creation. God uses particular people, times, places, and things in order to make his saving actions effective in people's lives. At its core, the sacramental worldview means that, instead of seeing creation as something opposed to God, we begin to see everything and every person God has created as the means by which he wants to share his life with us. To live a sacramental faith means that we have confidence that the physical can make the spiritual present and point toward it.

Second, a sacramental worldview means having a spiritual vision of the world and seeing everything through the eyes of eternity. The crux of faith means to see the world and its people as God sees them, through the eyes of Jesus. Everything has spiritual meaning if we only have the eyes to see. And other aspects of Christian life that God has established for us—the Bible, the Church, the lives and writings of the saints and Church Fathers, the devotions of the Church, the teachings of the magisterium, and so many other things—are all means by which God communicates his hidden will to us through what is tangible and created.

Third, the sacramental worldview is centered around participation. *Mystery* is the way we describe God's activity of drawing us into his life, our attempts to understand his activity in the world, and our response through the liturgical life of the Church. But participation can go even deeper. Saint Hilary, one of the Church Fathers, demonstrates this depth in his work on the Trinity when he describes our union with Christ:

> Now how it is that we are in him through the sacrament of the flesh and blood bestowed upon us, he himself testifies, saying, *And the world will no longer see me, but you shall see me; because I live you shall live also; because I am in my Father, and you in me, and I in you.* If he wished to indicate a mere unity of will, why did he set forth a kind of gradation and sequence in the completion of the unity, unless it were that, since he was in the Father through the nature of Deity, and we on the contrary in him through his birth in the body, he would have us believe that he is in us through the mystery of the sacraments? And thus there might be taught a perfect unity through a Mediator, while, we abiding in him, he abode in the Father, and as abiding in the Father abode also in us; and so we might arrive at unity with the Father, since in him who dwells naturally in the Father by birth, we also dwell naturally, while he himself abides naturally in us also.[1]

Here Saint Hilary takes it as a matter of fact that we dwell in Christ. While reflecting on the gift of the Eucharist, he emphasizes that it's no mere receiving of Jesus' Body but a means of dwelling with him through his Church. And yet, the Eucharist is just one means of participation. Saint Hilary

---

1. Philip Schaff and Henry Wace, eds., *A Select Library of Nicene and Post-Nicene Fathers of the Christian Church.* Second Series, vol. 9. E.W. Watson and L. Pullan, trans. (Buffalo, NY: Christian Literature Publishing Co., 1908), 141–142.

points out that Christ dwells in the Father by his divine nature, that we dwell in Christ because of his human nature, and that Christ dwells in us through the sacraments. Because Jesus links the realm of God and the realm of man as Mediator, he thereby brings the two into intimate communion and so brings us into communion with God. In short, the Christian life is participation, or "living in Christ."

To be a Christian means to share Jesus' life. It means that today we are really *participating* in the events and actions of Jesus' life. Our purpose as Christians is to rediscover the sacramental vision of our faith. But what are the benefits of developing this worldview? Simply this: it makes us more aware of God's action and love at work in our lives and in the lives of others. It helps us to attune our hearts to God's heart, and thereby to hear things according to God's register, rather than that of fallen humanity.

The sacramental worldview is a balm against the false ideologies that press upon us from all sides—especially the idea that the material cannot manifest the spiritual, that the visible cannot make known the invisible. The Christian vision is totally opposite. It gives the material world—God's creation—a power and dignity that no other worldview can supply. The sacramental worldview, then, builds up our understanding that the physical world does matter, because God has created it for us. Creation is not the end: God is. If we look at creation through the eyes of God, we see it as a sign that points us toward both our origin and goal: God.

The sacramental worldview also helps us see everything in the Church as alive and active. While we cannot discount the central importance of the historical character of our faith, theology, Scripture, and hierarchical structures are not historical artifacts that we study only to have a better sense of who we are today. Such study has its place, certainly, but it's limited. Rather, the sacramental worldview helps us see everything as imbued with God's presence here and now. God is active both through the forces of history and in the liturgy, in the Scriptures, and in the magisterium of the Church. If we take seriously the view that mystery means the activity of God always working to save us, this means that God is doing that today, right now. He's always at work: "My Father is at work until now, so I am at work" (Jn 5:17).

But let's be honest: we often fail to see the world and our faith sacramentally. Many of us easily question the need for liturgy and sacraments, for Mass, and for doctrine. They can seem so limiting and legalistic. Sometimes we can wonder if these concrete realities of time, place, smells, and bells are interfering with an authentic experience of God. Whether we recognize it or not, we've been formed in a culture and a worldview that is fundamentally opposed to a sacramental worldview. To clarify and make room for the idea that we participate in Christ through the Church, we must confront the ideology that says we do not need created things to encounter God. This ideology undermines the whole Christian worldview, never mind just the sacramental. Yet, culturally speaking, we are quite at home with this ideology. We breathe its air and often unconsciously allow it to shape much of the way we live our lives. This ideology is called modernism.

CHAPTER 3

Modernism: The Obstacle to the Sacramental Worldview

IF YOU SPEND ENOUGH TIME online, you'll most likely run into Catholics who refer to some Vatican II reforms as "modernist inventions." These people frequently use the word with special emphasis on the liturgical reform of the last fifty years. They often deem certain music and practices as "modernist" and accuse them of undermining the tradition of the Church. Yet this word is not reserved to liturgical debates. In the realm of theology, anything that goes beyond what some consider to be theological orthodoxy is often branded as "modern" and therefore a danger to the faith. Oftentimes, "modernism" is used by certain groups in the Church not so much to express a real theological and philosophical problem, but as a weapon to decry anything that conflicts with personal taste. The reason the term "modern" is misused by so many within the Church is that many Catholics do not have a deep understanding of the Church's magisterium and the precise meaning the magisterium gives to this word. In view of these misunderstandings, let's get to the heart of the meaning of modernism.

First, let's just consider the words on their own terms. Both "modern" and "modernism" have different connotations and can carry a lot of baggage. Sometimes "modern" refers to something new and is synonymous with the word "contemporary." Or the term refers to a particular style. For example, modern art puts an emphasis on technical precision over and against beautiful form. Thus, a modern building may be a technical achievement but might not look beautiful. In Catholic circles, the word is similarly loaded and often misused, as in the examples we've just looked at.

To put it simply, modernism is the denial of mediation. This may sound abstract, but if we reflect for a moment on the meaning of mediation, we can understand the consequences of the error of modernism. Mediation means that God is able to communicate with creation *through* his creation. To put it differently, the way God chooses to reveal himself is almost always *through* something or someone. How does God rescue Israel? *Through* the work of Moses. And how does God reveal himself to Moses? *Through* the burning bush. This is how God works with his creation.

In fact, one of the titles of Jesus is "Mediator" between God and man (see 1 Tim 2:5). Mediation in Catholicism, then, is the belief that God works both in and through his creation and that God and the whole of creation relate to and interact with one another. In other words, the "stuff" of creation is the means by which creation and God relate to each other. Creation's spiritual and material elements are the conduits through which we reach out to God and God reaches out to us. Modernism undermines mediation in the most fundamental way because it argues that God and creation *can't* interact with each other, that the physical and the spiritual are completely incompatible. In this way modernism is the denial of mediation.

Modernism has deep spiritual and intellectual implications. For instance, if God and the world cannot interact, then the universe could not have been created by God. Human beings could not have souls implanted in them directly by God, nor would God have been involved in their creation and formation. We'd also be stuck in this corruptible nature rather than destined for heaven. If Scripture is interpreted according to modernism, God could not be the active force that rescues the Israelites or chooses them as his specific people. The prophets could not foretell the Messiah because it would be impossible for God to speak through them. In fact, the litany of scriptural events modernism puts into question is endless: the virgin birth would be impossible; Jesus would only be a man and not also God; miracles would be impossible; the resurrection would become a myth invented by the apostles; the Holy Spirit would not descend upon the apostles at Pentecost. Modernism would say that the Scriptures are not inspired, the Church is not divinely instituted, and the sacraments are mere symbols at best. According to the modernist, faith is nothing more than a subjective feeling and prayer is an illusion. This litany is but a taste of what would happen if modernism were true, so it becomes clear why the Church fought—and is continuing to fight—against this worldview. If modernism is true, then Christianity is false. The danger is real.

Background

So, how did modernism creep into our way of thinking? While modernism began to make an appearance among some philosophers and theologians in the late Middle Ages, it took definitive form during the Rationalist and Enlightenment period, especially with philosophers such as René Descartes and Immanuel Kant. Each of these thinkers wanted to create a system of thought that depended solely on the human mind without any reference to the outside world. In other words, truth was no longer to be found through the world but determined solely by human reason. Unintentionally, these philosophers began to sow the intellectual roots of modernism by detaching reason from knowledge of truth through the external world. The consequences were vast, and they gradually shaped intellectual movements. This may seem abstract, but in reality this perspective has formed most people's way of thinking and has become part of the air we breathe.

Many modern ways of thinking about the world emphasize that truth cannot be discovered through things, which means that we do not have the ability to perceive the spiritual reality of the world through physical objects. The physical no longer points to the truth about creation, about God, and about who we are. *We* determine truth; truth is no longer revealed through creation.

Let's look at an example. As Christians, we believe that the human body reveals who we are. Our body and our person are intimately bonded together. We would say that we are created male and female, and that this fact is part of who we are. Thus, we cannot create our sexuality; it is really and truly a gift to us. However, some ideologies hold that to be male or female is a fluid concept and has no connection with the body. The Church, of course, recognizes real struggles that people have with gender dysphoria, but she also encourages us to regard masculinity and femininity as real and true gifts from God. Our bodies reveal a real aspect of our identity. But certain ideologies concerning gender and sexuality ignore the body and look to the self, to what one feels inside, as the only arbiter of truth. In this way, as in many others, modernism has infected not only forms of thinking, but even how we see ourselves as human beings. Most profoundly, it has infected how we understand our relationship with God.

Modernism began to impact the Church more directly in the nineteenth and early twentieth centuries, when a question began to arise in scriptural scholarship: *How can the miracles of Jesus be proven when we only have the biblical texts that say they happened? How do we know that Jesus actually said and did the things recorded in Scripture? How can we trust writers in their recounting of these stories?* Here, we can already perceive the influence of modernism. These questions presuppose that the Scriptures cannot be divinely inspired. If they were—in the eyes of these thinkers—then there would be no doubt about the veracity of Scripture, and readers would trust that the written words tell the truth about Jesus and the other events of both the Old and New Testaments. Instead, these scholars wanted to prove the events of the Bible with historical certainty. If they could not prove them, it would follow that either they did not happen or they were legends or fables that could be discounted as mythical and untrue.

These questions created shockwaves in Catholic scholarship and began to build to the point of an intellectual crisis in the Church.[1] Since Scripture was under a barrage of intellectual attacks, so too were theology and the deposit of faith. If the words of Scripture could be doubted, then so could all the teachings of the Church. For example, if the divinity of Jesus is put into serious doubt—as many of these scholars attempted to do—it throws into question most of Jesus' words and actions. If Jesus is only human and not also God, then Jesus is merely a man determined by his culture and without full freedom. This view had concrete implications for the way people thought about Church teaching. For instance, if Jesus' actions in choosing the twelve apostles are regarded as culturally determined, then this invites scrutiny around a male-only priesthood. Thinking this way also removes the divinely instituted elements of the Church and her hierarchy, leaving a purely human institution. Moreover, it removes all need for any hierarchical structure to the Church or, really, the need for the Church at all.

In the context of these debates, Pope Pius X brought the term "modernism" into prominence and spoke forcefully against it in his encyclical *Pascendi Dominici Gregis*.[2] Without giving a simple definition of modernism, the encyclical describes many of its characteristics: modernism encourages

---

1. Interestingly, it's in light of this crisis that a flurry of documents on the nature and meaning of Scripture were released, providing magisterial guidance in approaching the Scriptures with both faith and intellectual rigor.

2. Pope Pius X, *"Pascendi Dominici Gregis,"* http://www.vatican.va/content/pius-x/en/encyclicals/documents/hf_p-x_enc_19070908_pascendi-dominici-gregis.html.

atheism and agnosticism, views religion as a product of history rather than of God's intervention, reduces faith to experience with no connection to objective truth, and so much more.

Since the release of *Pascendi*, the Church has continued her fight against modernism. In fact, it was because of the filtering of modernism's ideology into the theological and practical life of the Church that the Second Vatican Council was called. The Council was an attempt to help the Church rediscover her sacramental reality and lived participation in Christ. It saw modernism as the danger it was: that it undermined the belief that God works with and through his creation to make himself known to his creatures. The Council, then, attempted to give the Church a direction forward. It wanted to provide the Church with a real and sustaining foundation for our participation in the life of Christ while also recognizing the lived and existential reality of modernism that every person in today's world experiences.

This brief foray into the heresy of modernism is meant to simply point out that modernism is very dangerous on multiple fronts. If modernism is the denial of mediation, then it is the denial that God acts in the world. Intuitively, we may already see how this has profound implications for the sacramental worldview. If God can't act in the world, then the whole idea that God uses creation to point us toward him and lift us into his life is foolishness. Furthermore, modernism also undermines fundamental aspects of being human. Therefore, in order to move forward, we must now look at what makes the modernistic worldview untrue and the sacramental worldview more reasonable.

An Argument Against Modernism

So how can we clear the shadow of modernism from our vision and begin to see Christian living much more accurately and more beautifully? To do this we need to engage in a discipline known as apologetics. In its simplest understanding, apologetics offers a defense. We want to offer a compelling defense for the Catholic sacramental worldview—which means we need to poke holes in modernism. Let's begin by asking some fundamental questions about life and exploring the Catholic response: *What does it mean to be human, and how do we function in the world?*

In order to answer these questions, we have to define a human being. Humans are a body-soul composite. We are material and spiritual creatures at the same time. The body has a particular purpose. When we see the body, we see the person; the body reveals a person in front of us. For this reason, we can say that the body is a sacrament: a visible sign that points to and makes real an invisible reality. This is part of God's original plan: he breathes life into humanity and thereby makes us living, spiritual beings. But this spiritual being is embodied, because the soul and the body have a deep connection. Death is so unnatural to us because it separates the soul from the body, and only in Christ's resurrection do we see the reunification of body and soul as God intended. Thus, Christians believe that at the end of time the soul will be reunited with the body. The body, then, is fundamentally good. It's something God always intends for us to have.

If the human person is a body-soul composite, and functions as such, this has a few implications. First, not only do human persons reveal their personhood—the invisible but real aspect of themselves—through their bodies, but they also reveal the presence of God. Being made in God's image and likeness, our humanity points to God and reveals him. The fact that we have reason and will, for example, is testimony not only to the fact that we are persons, but that we've been endowed with great gifts from God himself. This means that reason and will are not the products of evolution, but rather the result of God's creative activity. When he imbues us with a soul, he imbues us with the ability to relate to others, to reason, and to will. These faculties, in a mysterious way, point to the Creator who gave them to us. Human beings, then, make visible what cannot be seen: not only their personhood, but God himself.

What does this have to do with modernism? It's quite simple and straightforward: if human beings exist as embodied souls, if we are persons who show ourselves to others through our bodies, then this implies that we communicate spiritual and invisible truths in a visible and perceptible fashion. The human person exists in mediation! We mediate our person to the world—and even mediate God to the world. Because this is a basic fact of our humanity, it means that this is how we function as humans. If we use our bodies to manifest that we exist in and through our bodies, then this is how we communicate at all times.

On their most fundamental level, language and human expression work in a mediated fashion. We use words, signs, and gestures to communicate hidden and invisible ideas to others. We use words—written or spoken. We either see or hear words—they are perceptible. But they communicate something invisible to us: the *concepts* that the words attempt to communicate. When we say the word "rock," other people know exactly what we mean by that. The word is just some squiggles on a page or a noise that strikes our ear. But we as humans allow words to be signs that point us to invisible concepts.

On a daily basis, then, we work and function as creatures who mediate. To phrase this differently, it doesn't take long to see that fundamentally we are sacramental creatures. We use the physical and material in all our actions to manifest the invisible and the spiritual. We don't need to look any further than our own basic experience to see that this is true. On a purely human and natural level, sacramentality is how we function and move about in our lives.

This is why the Church herself has a sacramental structure and life. She doesn't have this as some sort of magical way of dispensing grace: rather, it's based on how the world itself is structured. Since to be human means to be naturally sacramental, Christ, taking all that is good and true about our humanity, builds upon this reality and imbues it with the life of grace and gives the sacraments as a gift to the Church. The Church takes material things to mediate God's presence to us and thereby communicate the life of grace to us in a way familiar to us. The sacramental worldview, then, is absolutely necessary in the life of the Christian because it is absolutely human.

Both in the life of the Church and in our natural human life, sacramentality depends on mediation in order to properly function. To be human is to be creatures that mediate invisible realities through material things. Modernism undermines what's most natural to us and creates a world where spirit and matter do not interact. The material world is its own domain, knowable only through scientific knowledge, and the spiritual is reduced to personal, interior experience.

According to this reasoning, if the material world cannot communicate the spiritual, if the material and spiritual are separated worlds that will never meet, then the material world has no sign value. This includes our bodies, our words, and our gestures: they have no meaning. Yet we know that we experience a deep desire for meaning. On the experiential level we can intuit our need for meaning and how the modernistic way of thinking can undermine it. If we take this loss of meaning to its logical conclusions, everything becomes a mere construct, something fabricated rather than imbued with purpose. At best, modernism merely allows us to construct our own meaning and to determine what our bodies and our language mean for us. But no real outside reference exists, no pointing beyond to greater and higher things. This reduces our spiritual horizons and makes it difficult to see God at work in the world. The spiritual aspect of humanity—if it's real at all—is something the mind cannot perceive because the body cannot communicate it. If this is what modernism entails, we can see how it not only affects our faith: it also affects how we experience our humanity! Modernism is an attack on the very foundation of what it means to be human.

What we have attempted here is by no means exhaustive. We are beginning to lay bare the fundamental flaw of modernism: it's an affront to our human experience. Deep down, we know that the material world can communicate what is invisible. We see it function day by day. When a child points at a four-legged furry animal running across a field and yells "dog," we know exactly what the child means. Our eyes seeing the dog the child points at, our ears hearing that tiny voice scream, communicate to us that a dog is truly there. A similar process is also happening right now as you read the words in this book. We apprehend the invisible only by and through the visible. This is the basic fact that we must remember.

The sacramental vision of Christianity makes a lot more sense when it's put into dialogue with our basic human experience. We must remind ourselves of this reality if we want to draw closer to God. God works *through* creation and uses it to help point us toward him because that's how we are constituted as human beings. He approaches us through sacraments and the Church. If we can begin to internalize this, then modernism will start to loosen its grip on our lives and the sacramental vision of Christianity will truly begin to take root in our hearts.

Keeping all this in mind as we move forward, we need to build up the truth of this sacramental vision. This is not an easy task. It means developing a new way of seeing the world, the faith, the Church, God—pretty much everything! Our purpose here has been to situate ourselves in our historical moment and our experience, to see how we live within the context of modernism and how this ideology is an affront to our human experience. Knowing this, we have begun to clear away the false ideas that hinder us from clearly seeing the riches of our faith and what the Church offers us in Christ.

How Modernism Seeps into Our Lives

You might be wondering, "All this talk about modernism is well and good, but how can I know whether this way of thinking is actually playing out in my life?" Indeed, it's important to recognize some of the ways modernism seeps into our lives so we can internalize and see that this isn't just some academic debate among theologians and philosophers: this ideology can have a profound impact on the Christian life. Doctrine—teachings that all Catholics are obliged to believe—influences life. And life influences doctrine. The same goes for philosophy and ideologies. Therefore, it's important for us to understand that whether we realize it or not, modernism almost certainly impacts our spiritual vision of reality.

First, modernism seeps into our lives when it undermines our belief in the reality and power of the sacraments. When we question, for instance, whether it's possible for God to turn bread into the sacramental Presence of Jesus. Or whether a priest can really forgive sins. The most common question priests get asked is, "Why do I have to confess my sins to a priest? Can't I just confess them to God directly?" Putting to one side Jesus' transfer to the Church of his authority to forgive sins (see Jn 20:23), we can clearly see the denial of mediation in this question. Modernism makes it difficult for us to understand that God uses mediators—in this case priests—to be ministers of forgiveness. A sacramental vision, on the other hand, makes it clear that God works through people like priests in order to make his grace effective.

Modernism's spell may even be more subtle. Let's take an example popular in both Protestant and Catholic circles: to make a life decision for Jesus. Often, faith is presented as an individual choice. Many who preach the Gospel emphasize what Christ has done for us, what his cross and resurrection have effected, and urge that to receive salvation we simply need to give our lives over to Christ today. Seems pretty harmless, right? And, indeed, this is not *bad*, but it's an insufficient way of preaching the faith. Notice that faith is unmediated? It's all about personal choice, directly with Jesus. But something essential is missing—the Church. Modernism sees no problem with the above presentation, but the Catholic position must always include the Church because the Church is the place of faith. We gain faith *through* the Church! Yes, there is a real moment of decision in the life of every Christian, but it's not an individualistic decision for faith. It's an assent to the grace offered through the Church, Christ's body, to which we are united.

Finally, a great spiritual malady connected to modernism that affects humanity today is the sin known as acedia. Acedia is known in Western Christianity as "sloth," but it is more than mere laziness. One pithy way to describe acedia is that it entices us away from desiring the good. At the heart of this sin is the temptation to avoid particular goods for both ourselves and others. It can express itself in myriad ways. It is at play when you know you ought to pray but instead check your phone, when your kids need you to make dinner and all you want to do is read a good book, when things aren't going well in your marriage and you look at religious life and think "my life would have been better as a priest or a nun." Acedia attempts to remove our focus from the good in front of us at a particular moment and make us yearn for greener pastures. This is why acedia is not just laziness: it is, at its heart, the sin of avoidance.

How are modernism and acedia connected? Modernism says, "We can't encounter God through particular things" and acedia says, "Avoid the particular things through which we encounter God." They are two sides of the same coin: both refuse to find God in the particular and material stuff of life. Obviously, acedia is not the fruit of modernism, since it is an ancient way of describing a particular affliction of the soul. But we can say that acedia has a spiritual affinity with the attitudes that develop with modernism. Every time we give in to this sin, it chips away at our desire for the good—both the particular goods of life and the ultimate good found in God. In fact, acedia often focuses on particular goods because they are the very means that point us toward our ultimate good and goal in God. Acedia doesn't want us to desire God and therefore doesn't want us to desire the particular goods of life. By not desiring the goods, we lose our desire for the Good. Acedia is a sin that attempts to reduce desire. And this reduction of our desire makes it more and more difficult to see God. We begin to doubt that he's really active and present—not just in our lives, but in the world. Acedia is sinister because it so easily and frequently attacks the very things that help us find God—which is how this connects with the concept of sacramentality. The particular and material stuff of our lives—our vocations, our families, our missions, our jobs—all of these are the means by which we encounter God. Acedia tempts us to believe these are barriers to our discovery of God. We think, "If only I didn't have to tend to my children, I'd have more time for prayer; if only I didn't have to deal with that difficult co-worker, I'd have more Christian charity." Acedia wants us to avoid the gifts of specific moments and people in our lives. Thus, it removes the very means that God provides for becoming saints.

God works *through* people, places, and situations to make himself present to us. By eroding these connections, acedia ultimately tempts us away from the concrete situations, people, and places through which we can come to encounter God. When we stop searching for God in these things, we close ourselves to the opportunity to encounter him. We train ourselves to think that God is not found *through* particular things, but rather that God, if he is to be found, can only be discovered when we *remove* these things from our lives. And this outlook begins to train us in other spiritual attitudes. If we can't find God in the particular places, people, and situations of our lives, then temptation arises around the sacraments themselves. We think, "I am not getting anything out of the sacraments, the liturgy, prayer, Scripture, living the Gospel" and so on. We may desire God in some sense, but we even begin to doubt that he is at work in the sacramental and liturgical life of the Church. If we can't find God in the particular things of our lives, it becomes difficult to find him in the particulars of the sacramental life of the Church. This in turn begins to undermine our ability to find him at work in history and the world today. Our prayer life begins to falter, our faith is increasingly pushed to the side, and our belief in God begins to fade.

The good news, though, is that we are not left to float aimlessly in a world that wants to deprive us of the encounter with God. God is real, he is active, and he is drawing us to himself through the life of faith. It is the Church that is the "place" of faith, the place where we encounter God. What the Church is, and how she is central to the life of faith, is the starting point for finding God anew through this sacramental lens, because the Church *is* the sacrament of Christ's presence to the world!

PART TWO

The Sacramental Worldview
and the Church

CHAPTER 4

The Church as the Place of Faith

I WAS BAPTIZED CATHOLIC AS an infant, but while my parents were really loving, faith just wasn't a priority growing up. There was nothing intentional about it. My mother, the Catholic of the family, was often quite ill from post-polio complications while I was growing up. So, I was never really raised in the faith; I never even received my first Communion! However, when I went to university, something happened to bring faith to the forefront. I needed to find a place to stay and was getting a little desperate because I hadn't looked into it ahead of time. Then my grandma called me and said she had read in her church bulletin that a priest had rooms for rent for Catholic men attending university. Now, as you can probably imagine, living with a priest was not at the top of my to-do list as a young man about to move out on his own for the first time. But I needed a place to live. So, I moved in with Father John and another university student.

During my first year at university, I went to Mass a couple times and believed I was being a good Catholic but didn't think much about it. Then I ended up staying with Father John during the summer because I was taking some summer classes. One night, I was invited to a movie, and the seminarian we went with happened to ask me when I received my Confirmation and first Communion. I said, "What are those?" Father John soon invited me to attend RCIA to learn about the faith and to seek out the rest of my sacraments of initiation. I didn't have much interest, but I thought, "I suppose this wouldn't hurt," so I attended and received the sacraments at the Easter Vigil that year. But I was too afraid so I never made my first confession and stopped going to Mass the Sunday after Easter.

I returned to Victoria for my third year of university, ready to try a new program. I received the odd e-mail from Father John wondering how I was doing and asking why he hadn't seen me at Mass, but I would just come up with a lie or excuse. Deep down I just didn't care. But then a little less than a year later everything changed. I was sitting at my computer and for some reason I had a sudden need and desire to pray. Not knowing, really, how to pray, I simply closed my eyes and said Jesus' name slowly, over and over. It wasn't long afterward that I experienced God's love for me; I understood in a deep way that I was immersed in the life of God, that this was *the* fact of my life. It was overwhelming and I didn't know what to do. After this experience of prayer ended, I picked up my dusty Bible. I had never even cracked it open until that moment. I randomly opened to 1 Samuel 3: the call of Samuel. I immediately understood this to be a clear sign from God that my experience of his love in prayer was no fluke. God was calling me to himself in a real encounter.

I contacted Father John and asked him if I could return to RCIA and take it more seriously and he agreed. A few weeks in, we listened to a talk on confession. I expressed my hesitations but later that evening Father John said, "Sometimes you just need to bite the bullet." I took his advice seriously, did an examination of conscience, and lined up for Saturday morning confessions. I still feel sorry for the people in line that day because I was in there for a long time. But I walked out of the confessional feeling like a new man. Christ had really forgiven me. I was close to him. My life was his, and he lived his life out in me.

Reflecting on this experience, I see that it was the Church that brought this all about for me. My parents got me baptized and brought me into the life of faith; my grandma called me suggesting where to live. Father John patiently guided and encouraged me to grow closer to Jesus. While the conversion experience was a private moment, it was certainly the fruit of my Baptism and the countless prayers of persons in heaven and on earth. Even the Bible, which was so instrumental in my conversion, was compiled and authorized through the Church's ability to decide what is and isn't part of the canon of Scripture. Finally, the sacrament of confession, the crescendo of my whole experience, was the sacrament whereby my sins were forgiven, the life of grace was restored to me, and I became an active member of Christ's body, the Church. Without the Church, I would not be a practicing Catholic today. Without the Church, I would not be a priest today.

This is why I know not just intellectually but very deeply from experience that we must talk about the Church before we talk about the personal nature of faith. Without the

Church, we cannot have a personal relationship with Jesus; without the Church, we cannot have faith. Christ instituted his Church as the place where we come to encounter him, live in him, and know him. We cannot talk about Christ without his Church because, as Saint Paul reminds us in his writings, the Church is the body of Christ. To ignore the Church is to ignore Christ.

This discussion of the Church in connection with faith is often difficult for many Christians to wrap their minds around. For a variety of reasons, people may see faith in a more individualistic way: "Faith is my choice for Jesus." This view of faith, in which all that matters is my choice for Jesus, creates problems that undermine a sacramental worldview. For one, it makes us the sole judges of what is the true faith. Thus, we see our own vision of Jesus' identity as above and beyond that of the magisterium—the Church's teaching office. We struggle to see how "The Church"—with all the ominous tones it carries with it—really has anything to do with Jesus. We may not recognize it, but the modernism we spoke of in the last chapter often creates an obstacle to seeing the Church as central to the life of faith. If modernism is true, then obviously faith is a personal choice, with each individual the sole judge as to what the true faith entails. But if the sacramental vision is true, then the Church is actually vital—nay, essential—to the life of faith. Without the Church, the sacramental worldview we are proposing falls apart. This is why we want to investigate the Church in this chapter and the next: to see why the Church is essential for the Christian, to see that it is in and through the Church that we encounter God and are lifted up into his life.

This idea of needing a community of faith, structures, and authority does strongly clash with our modern sensibilities. We have an inherited distaste for basically anything that suggests authority over us. This is the air of modernism and we must be attuned to the subtle and, often, not-so-subtle ways it undermines the basic aspects of humanity. As we are going to see, institution, authority, and sacraments make the Church what she is: they are essential to her because they are essential to the flourishing of human life.

If individualism runs rampant in the Church, then we have a Church that is constantly at war. Wars of particular agendas, what certain people want or think is best for the Church, become commonplace. When people try to impose their own particular will on the Church, it's often a sign that they haven't gone through the crucifixion of their wills whereby they submit to Christ and allow his truth to purify them. Real Christian unity flows from communion—a unity of individuals with one common purpose and goal, albeit expressed in unique and individual ways. This is the heart of Christianity. In other words, Catholicism puts the emphasis on the "we" without destroying the "I." And because the "we" has a certain precedence, there must be a place where Christians come together to express themselves as a united body. This is what we call the Church: the "we" of the Christian people. Only in this "we" of the Church can we discover Christ. Without the Church, there is no relationship with Christ. The Church manifests Christ and makes him present to us individually, to all Christians together, and to the entire world. In other words, the Church is the sacrament whereby Christ is known, encountered, and loved.

The Place of Faith

If you've ever been to an infant Baptism, this scene will be all too familiar. At the beginning of the liturgy, the priest greets the parents, godparents, and child at the front of the church. The priest asks the parents a simple question, "What do you ask of God's Church?" The question the priest asks is vitally important and in a way is the first formation in the faith of the child. The parents can give one of two responses. The first is the most common. The parents often respond by saying "Baptism"—probably because it's easy to remember, since that's literally what's about to happen! But the ritual gives a second option also. Instead of "Baptism" the parents can answer "faith."

These answers tell us something important: Baptism and faith—the sacraments and our life in Christ—are given to us through the Church. It may seem odd that Baptism, given through the Church, is the means by which a child receives faith. After all, how does the Church give faith to a child? The problem is that unfortunately faith is often seen as an individual choice with no real connection to the Church, rather than as a gift and virtue given to us by God in Baptism. Faith isn't about me or you individually. Just as Baptism draws us into the Church and into communion with each other in Christ, faith is the whole Church living in Christ together. Faith is the Church's way of being.

What, then, is faith? It is a gift from God given to us through the Church which enables us to give ourselves totally to God and believe everything he has revealed. It's a theological virtue, which means that it is lived out in us by the grace given to us through the Church and through Baptism. It's not something earned, it's something received. It allows us to live in God's life and to allow God to dwell in us. Faith, then, is an invitation from God to participate in his life through the Church. Faith is more than belief, it's an ability to say "yes" to God with our whole life and thereby to allow God to dwell and live actively in us through Christ. We cannot achieve this on our own; the very ability to respond to God with our life comes from faith.

Let's bring this a step further into sacramentality. If faith is a gift given us through the sacrament of Baptism that brings us into the life of the Church, then this is the means by which the Christian faithful begin their sacramental life. Baptism saves us by virtue of Christ's cross made present in the sacrament, and it is in this saving action that God also reveals himself to the individual Christian as Father, Son, and Holy Spirit. In Baptism, the Christian is lifted up into God's life through Christian living in the Church. Baptism is the entry point to the sacramental worldview, and this vision of the world that is given us by faith is lived out only in the Church.

What Is the Church?

Often for Catholics, the word "Church" implies the clergy, the magisterium, the bishops, the Vatican, etc. Of course, these are all aspects of the Church, but they are not the whole Church. The Church is the society of all baptized Christians in the world. If one is baptized, one is a member of the Church of Christ. Thus, the Church does not act according to the whims of specific baptized people; the Church is a single subject—the one body of Christ. Since a real connection exists between the Church and Christ, this means that the Church is the principal place where Christ acts in the life of Christians. The Church is the meeting place between those who have faith in Christ and Christ himself. We may say that the Church is a singular actor. This means that it is through the Church that Christ works to make his saving grace efficacious in the lives of Christians.

If faith is a gift given to Christians by God in Christ Jesus, then the place it makes the most sense for this to occur is the Church. Think about it for a moment. Faith is made possible through the mediator between God and humanity: Jesus Christ. The Church is the body of Christ on earth, so it only makes sense that our union with him would take place in the Church. Through Baptism we come to Christ as members of his body, and the Church is where faith is given to Christians. This means, then, that God doesn't simply dispense the gift of faith to us in a direct fashion, according to a "me and Jesus" model of faith. Rather, faith is mediated through the Church to each individual believer. Remember: the word mediation is vital for the sacramental worldview. God chooses to work *through* his creation, and this also means through his Church. The Church is the mediator between God and the world, the middle point through which God and the world come together. God gives each one of us faith through the Church. If we want faith, we must have the Church.

But how do we know that this is God's plan? To put it rather simply, after his resurrection Jesus intimately identifies himself with the Church. On the road to Damascus, Jesus asks Saul, "Why are you persecuting *me*?" (Acts 9:4, emphasis added). We know, however, that Saul has been persecuting

Jesus' followers, not Jesus himself. So in these words we see very clearly that Jesus views the persecution of Christians as a persecution of himself. In the Gospel of Matthew, Jesus also identifies himself with the hungry, the thirsty, the naked by saying, "Whatever you did for one of these least brothers of mine, you did for me" (see Mt 25:40). These sayings in the New Testament prove fundamental for the early Church's understanding of the nature and meaning of the Church. They are what laid the foundations for Saint Paul to call the Church "the body of Christ."

The Gospel of John, too, is rich with images and parables in which Jesus describes the intimacy he has with his followers. In his Johannine commission, Jesus tells the disciples "As the Father has sent me, so I send you" (20:21). Throughout the Gospel of John, Jesus expresses a real union between the disciples and himself. His commission gives them an imperative: they are sent as he is sent. This implies, then, that they share in his mission. Just as Jesus is sent for the salvation of the world through the cross, so now the Church is sent along the same path. On this journey, Christ continues to live out his cross and resurrection through the members of the Church. Throughout the New Testament it's abundantly clear: if you want Jesus, you must have the Church. The two are so intimately tied that to lose one is to lose the other. Thus, since Christ gives the gift of faith, and the Church and Christ are so intimately connected, Christ will always give the grace and gift of faith through his body the Church, because the Church shares in his same mission.

This is why the Second Vatican Council said that the Church is like a sacrament: "Since the Church is in Christ

like a sacrament or as a sign and instrument both of a very
closely knit union with God and of the unity of the whole
human race, it desires now to unfold more fully to the faithful of the Church and to the whole world its own inner nature
and universal mission."[1] The Church makes visible to the
world the unity between God and man: it is the place where
Christ is intimately close with humanity, and the Council
uses the word "sacrament" to illustrate this closeness.

To summarize what we've discussed so far, faith is not so
much a personal form of belief as an entering into Christ. To
do this, we must be part of his body, the Church, in order to
have faith ourselves. We could say that the Church is the place
where faith resides, so if we want faith, we must be in the
Church. Faith, then, is more of a way of seeing than a simple
assent of the mind to the truths of God, though it's that too.
Faith sees the world through the eyes of Jesus; faith gives us
the ability to be in Jesus and to see, act, feel, think in him. In
other words, faith allows Christ to live in me. Faith is Christ
living in me—Christ acting, thinking, seeing, feeling in me.
This is summarized by Saint Paul when he writes, "I live, no
longer I, but Christ lives in me" (Gal 2:20). But faith is not
only Christ living in me; faith also allows me to live in Christ.
And Christ, as seen above, is identified with his Church,
making the Church the real place and center of faith.

How is this connected with the sacramental worldview?
Besides the fact that the Church is like a sacrament, faith itself
has a sacramental structure. Faith uses something visible
—Christ's body, the Church—to lift up the Christian into

---

1. *Lumen Gentium*, no. 1.

the very life of God. Faith, therefore, is just as much about body as it is about soul because it addresses both our visible and invisible natures. In the life of the Church, through faith, we are fed daily so that what we see, hear, taste, touch, and smell becomes the means by which God continuously feeds and builds up our life of faith. Think about the sacraments. Every single sacrament has something physical or perceptible about it, and it's through these perceptible signs that God truly communicates his life to us: he lifts us up into it! This is all God's work in the Church to help immerse us in the life of Jesus, to build up our faith, which is nothing other than sharing in the life of Jesus Christ. Faith is Jesus' way, through his Church, of making himself present to us in the most intimate way possible at every moment and in every place. Faith is everything because it's the new life given us by Baptism.

Faith, then, is allowing the mystery of Jesus' life to work in us, allowing ourselves to be conformed to him more closely, to become living icons of Christ in the world, to become saints. This is why the Church is so vital. Without the Church, we cannot become saints. Without the Church, we cannot be immersed in the mystery of Jesus' life, death, and resurrection. Without the Church, we have no means of accessing the saving gifts Jesus offered us two thousand years ago. Without the Church, salvation is impossible.[2] Seeing the vital role the Church plays in faith, we are better positioned to understand

---

2. See *Catechism of the Catholic Church*, nos. 1257–1261 and Second Vatican Ecumenical Council, *Gaudium et Spes*, no. 22, https://www. vatican.va/archive/hist_councils/ii_vatican_council/documents/ vat-ii_const_19651207_gaudium-et-spes_en.html.

her essential characteristics, and how the Church is the very heart of our sacramental vision.

Why the Church?

It's important to discuss, at least in brief, whether Jesus chose to institute a Church and, if so, why? It's a common mentality among many Christians to see the Church as running interference in the life of faith: "I don't need the Church, I have Jesus" is a common refrain. We have seen why the Church is necessary for faith, but that still doesn't answer the question of why Jesus sets things up this way. Why does he need a Church at all? Especially today, we have a strong dislike of organized bodies and institutions. We see them as crusty, old, and unnecessary. This is why so many people can be biased against the Church. Why would God want an institution?

To answer this we need to look to the very beginning of Jesus' ministry: "This is the time of fulfillment. The kingdom of God is at hand. Repent, and believe in the Gospel" (Mk 1:15). Over and over, throughout the Gospels, we hear Jesus preaching about his kingdom. Let's think for a moment about what a kingdom entails: a ruler, subjects, territory, buildings, infrastructure, institutions, etc. When Jesus is preaching about the Kingdom of God, he is saying that it's near for us to belong to. Thus, the Church is the place of Christ's reign. Indeed, as *Lumen Gentium* says, the Church is "the kingdom of Christ already present in mystery."[3]

---

3. *Lumen Gentium*, no. 72

Jesus' intention to found the Church finds further proof in Matthew's Gospel when Jesus says to Peter, "You are Peter, and upon this rock I will build my church" (Mt 16:18). Also, the epistles contain an array of references to the Church: the reference in 1 Peter 2:10 to Christians as "God's people," the many references by Saint Paul to the Church as the body of Christ, the analogy between marriage and Christ's love for his Church in Ephesians 5, etc. Overall, the word "Church" appears sixty-two times in Saint Paul's writings alone, along with many other allusions, words, and images relating to the Church.

Finally, in all of this we cannot forget the Old Testament. It's fairly clear that God establishes Israel as a people. The covenant promised to Israel isn't received on an individualistic basis; rather, it's clear from reading the Old Testament that Israel is a people who live a common life together, who follow the law together, and who partake in various rituals together. It would be odd for God to see this as necessary for Israel, but unnecessary for the Christian. In fact, this is one of the reasons that Jesus chooses twelve apostles: they are symbolic of the twelve patriarchs of Israel. This is why one of the titles of the Church is the New Israel. If the Old Testament is meant to prepare and foreshadow what comes in the new, then what is in the old is not abolished but fulfilled. Jesus intends to establish a Church, which is the fulfillment of what God began in Israel. Thus, there need to be common teachings, a common scripture, a teaching authority, and patriarchs upon which the Church is to find her continuity and stability. Israel is not annulled by the establishment of the Church, but rather brought to fulfillment. Hence Jesus' words: "Do not think that I have come to abolish the law or the prophets. I have come not to abolish but to fulfill" (Mt 5:17).

Even from this brief overview, it becomes obvious that Jesus intended and established a Church. From the beginning, Jesus allowed for an institutional element to be a part of the Church. The role of the apostles in Acts gives countless examples of their need to govern and to decide various matters for the good of the whole Church. It is human and natural to have institutions, to have organizational structures. No "pure spiritual church" exists, for the simple reason that we aren't pure spiritual beings. We also must remember that, while redeemed, we are still all sinners and that some people attempt to set the flock of Christ astray through false teaching and immoral behavior. There has to be a government for the sake of unity, so the Church can live her mission as a sacrament of salvation. If there are no institutions, then we are lacking something fundamental to our common humanity, and therefore we aren't living sacramentality in a serious fashion.

The Church, then, was something Christ wilfully chose to extend his kingdom to all the earth, and he established it to continue even after his ascension. The Church exists to make Christ present throughout all of history; it's his body at work in the world through its members, that is, the baptized. Jesus established it to be the place where we encounter him so as to grow close to him. Also, he established it to be visible to the world, so that those who do not yet believe can encounter him through his Church. He further established structures and laws and set aside men for the purpose of ensuring the

Church's unity. This is necessary for the Church's sacramental life and for her own existence as a sacrament. At this point one might ask: what are the essential characteristics of the Church? This is a question that we will explore in the next chapter. By exploring these characteristics, we will begin to see how necessary they are for our participation in the life of Christ.

CHAPTER 5

The Church as Communion

AFTER THE SECOND VATICAN COUNCIL, there was a debate based on *Lumen Gentium*, the Council's document on the Church, as to what the primary image of the Church should be. One particular vision took the Council's idea of the Church as the "People of God." This is an important image, especially in connection with the Old Testament, but it got usurped as a sort of political vision in which the people took charge of the Church's leadership. Some foresaw a more democratic Church and the need to abolish any concept of hierarchy. These voices took a particular image of the Church that the Council rightly used, but removed it from its context to serve a particular political and theological agenda.

This is only one example of some of the turmoil that occurred after the Council. Eventually Cardinal Ratzinger intervened. In 1995 he issued a clarification in which he stated that the Church, as presented in the theology of the Second Vatican Council, is best interpreted as a hierarchical communion, and that any other images from the conciliar documents ought to be read through that lens. It was a clarifying moment that helped the Church move forward in her understanding of how to bring the whole Church, that is, all the baptized, into a healthy unity with the clergy and other authority structures. This image balanced out the need for both laity and clergy and saw them as intended by the Lord himself when he established the Church. Most fundamentally, this idea that the Church is a hierarchical communion builds up and supports the view that the Church is herself a sacrament.

The Church as the Universal Sacrament of Salvation

The Second Vatican Council called the Church the Universal Sacrament of Salvation. Let us take into account everything we've said about sacrament so far and apply it to the Church. This will help us understand the role and purpose of some of the other elements of the Church, especially those aspects we often think limit our ability to encounter Jesus. By recognizing the Church as the universal sacrament of salvation, we see that such elements as hierarchy, authority, and magisterium are at the service of presenting Christ to the world.

Sacramentality refers to something perceptible that is a sign of a particular reality and makes that reality present. Sacramentality, then, effects what it signifies and gives persons who partake of these various sacramental realities the ability to be lifted to Christ and participate in Christ. So, if the Church is the universal sacrament of salvation, she makes visible and perceptible the salvation of humanity. To say this differently, the Church makes visible Jesus' death and resurrection. We cannot see this mystery directly, but it's possible to encounter it and see it through the Church and, in fact, this is the Church's principal mission and role. Everything about the Church—her liturgy, her sacraments, her hierarchy, the mission of the laity, etc.—all serve this mission of the Church to make visible the salvation given by Jesus, to serve her mission to be the universal sacrament of salvation.

This sacramental understanding of the Church is the proper light by which to view the Church's various features and contours. Jesus constituted his Church with a very specific structure so as to ensure that his mission of salvation could be continued. This mission of salvation occurs through the Church in which Christ makes himself present to the world.

Not only does the Church make Christ present to the world, but she also is the place where the drama of salvation takes center stage. This means that we her members will never be perfect: the effects of sin remain in us, and God is slowly working to purify us of these effects. Thus, the Church is going to contain elements of sinfulness, even though in and of herself she is always holy. The Church is holy in her Founder, sinful in her members. The Church is the place where God is attempting to make us holy by drawing us more deeply into his life through our mysterious participation in his cross. This mystery is always at work, always active, always trying to draw us deeper into communion with the Trinity.

Why mention this? If the Church is the universal sacrament of salvation, if she makes the redemptive mystery of

Christ visible to the world, then when her members—lay and clergy alike—are sinful, this creates a sort of anti-sacrament that hinders people outside the Church from recognizing their savior. Jesus is all holy, but none of the members of the Church are sinless: this is the very reason we're in the Church! We need Jesus to draw us to participate in his cross so that we can die to sin and share in his resurrection.

It's always important to keep this paradox of holiness and sinfulness in mind in regard to the Church, so we can recognize what is essential and not allow sinfulness to muddy the Church's mission. On the other hand, this must also inspire us to holiness: we have to recognize that insofar as we allow sin to reign, we are doing a disservice to the Church's mission by making it difficult for others to find Christ through her. The more we are united together in the faith, the more we make Christ visible to the world.

This oneness is at the heart of the Church's life, and is essential for the sacramental worldview, because if we are united with one another that allows Christ to be more visible. Christ knows that when there is unity in the Church, when she is truly one and universal, she reflects the unity of the Trinity: "may all be one . . . that the world may believe that you sent me" (Jn 17:21). Notice how Jesus makes the connection between unity and belief? He knows that the Church has the opportunity to reveal the love of God to the world, but she does this most perfectly when she is united.

Yet this unity does not ignore diversity. Just as God is one God in three Persons—Father, Son, and Holy Spirit—so is the Church one Church in a variety of members and rites. Such variety is not subversive to the unity of the Church;

rather, it's what guarantees her unity and allows the various ritual and cultural differences, along with varying differences of theological emphasis, to be the full expression of the height, length, breadth, and depth of Christ himself. The one Church of Christ consists of all the baptized faithful, and those who are in communion with Rome—whether they be Latin, Byzantine, Ruthenian, or belong to any of the many other Catholic Rites—find themselves in the fullness of what Jesus intended his Church to be. In fact, the Pope is the principle of unity for the Church: to be in union with Rome is to be in union with all that Christ intended the Church to be in her essential structure. If the Church is a sacrament, then, she is an entity that unifies different Christians into one body confessing one and the same faith. This unity is the principal means by which the Church witnesses to the world about Christ's salvation. The more holy and united the Church is, the more she makes Christ visible to the world.

Apostolic Succession: Guarantee of Sacramentality

What is common to the fullness of Christ's Church— what really constitutes her as a Church—are two basic elements: apostolic succession and sacramental life. These are the common threads that ensure the unity of the Church and, therefore, her mission.

The bishops are the successors of the apostles. Every bishop in the world can trace his line of succession all the way back to the apostles. The bishops exist to help ensure unity in the local churches—known as dioceses—where they exercise the roles of teaching, governing, and sanctifying the faithful of their particular territory. The Church cannot exist without bishops, since the bishops guarantee the validity of our sacraments. Bishops exist not only to ensure the unity of their local churches, but also to ensure that we receive the sacraments as Christ intended them.

To illustrate this, let's consider the sacrament of Holy Orders. We cannot have sacraments without bishops and priests, and both bishops and priests depend on other bishops to ordain them. If there are no bishops, then, outside of Baptism, we would really have no sacraments. This is why we state that the Church has these two key features: bishops who guarantee the unity of the Church with her ability to participate in the sacramental life, and the sacraments themselves, which are Christ's way of uniting us more intimately with his body, the Church.

The Church's membership comprises both clergy and laity. This division, which intends a clear line of authority culminating in the Pope, is called the hierarchy of the Church. But the two parts are always at the service of one another. This is why we also say that in addition to being a hierarchy the Church is a communion: it's a communion of loving service between all members in the various orders and states of life to serve the common good, which is building up the Church.

This entails, too, that the Church will always have an institutional component. Institutions are a human reality, and as we have been at pains to explain in this book, God uses the most human things to reveal himself to the world. This is no less true for the Church. She must have institutional elements such as laws, structures, and governance because these are part of any human society, and the Church is herself a particular society of Christian faithful. We so often stick up our noses at the thought of institutions, but the fact remains that from her earliest days the Church was governed, had laws, and so on, in order to guarantee that the common good of all the faithful would be attained.

The Sacraments: Ordinary Means of Participating in the Life of Christ

The second essential aspect which flows from the guarantee of apostolic succession is the Church's sacramental life. The sacraments are the ordinary means of grace, though grace is not limited to the sacraments only. The bishops exist to order the Church in such a way as to ensure that the ordinary means of grace are available to the faithful as much as possible. Each sacrament's primary effect is to unite us in a unique way to Christ, thus building up the unity of his body, the Church.

Each sacrament brings this to fruition differently. Baptism brings us into the Church and unites us to Christ in a definitive way that cannot be revoked. This is what we mean when we say that Baptism places an indelible mark on the receiver: our relationship with God in Christ has changed permanently. Confirmation likewise effects a permanent change; in Confirmation our unity with the Church is completed and, in receiving more abundantly the grace of the Holy Spirit, we are united to the Church in her missionary endeavors to make Christ present to the world. The Eucharist is the sacramental presence of Jesus: he is truly present in his body, blood, soul, and divinity under the appearance of bread. By giving this gift in the Mass, Jesus offers himself totally to the world. We Christians who receive the Eucharist receive the particular grace of being united to the Church, both to those alive who are receiving and those gone before us who reign with Christ in heaven. By receiving his Body, we become more united to his body, the Church.

Confession, as a sacrament of healing, restores a unity that has been broken through sin. By the merits of Christ's death on the cross, confession heals the sinner and forgives the sin, thereby reuniting the penitent with the body of Christ. If the person committed any mortal sin, he or she is now free to receive Communion once more, which is thus a sign of lived unity with the whole Church. The other sacrament of healing, the Anointing of the Sick, unites a person's sufferings to Christ and the Church. In a unique way, through this sacrament sufferings become a means by which Jesus works his salvation for the world: thus, because of the fruits of their suffering, the sick help build up the unity of the Church.

In Marriage we witness the sacrament of Christ's love for his Church and the Church's love for Christ. The marriage ceremony clearly shows that the unity of the couple is a sacrament—a living and real sign—of Christ's unity with his Church: as a husband and wife are one, so Christ and his Church are one. Thus, in its unity Christian Marriage witnesses to this deep and intimate unity between Christ and his Church; it also witnesses to the necessity of the Church for the world to receive and see Christ's love.

The sacrament of Holy Orders has a threefold ministry of deacon, priest, and bishop. Each order plays a particular role in building up the unity of the Church. The deacon's role is to build up this unity through the service of charity by ministering to those in need, both within the Church and outside, in a way that differs from that of the laity. The deacon's indelible mark received at ordination allows him to bring Christ in a special way to those in need because in his person he makes present Christ the Servant. The priest's principal role is to celebrate the sacraments, pray for the people, and teach them about the faith. By virtue of his particular ministries he shares in the ministry of the bishop. In offering the sacraments that unify, his very priesthood exists to draw people into deeper communion with Christ and his Church. The liturgical life, of which the priests and bishops are the main celebrants, leads the whole Church into its union with Christ and draws them daily into communion with him.

In all of this we see the various ways Christ lifts us up into his life, including the particular ways the sacraments bring this about. But, as stated earlier, while the sacraments are the ordinary means of grace, they are not the only means of grace. The grace of Christ is always offered to all baptized Christians in order to unite us with his life, and this always happens through the Church.

The Church as the Place of Participation in Christ

At the heart of everything that's been said, one thing has hopefully become abundantly clear: to have access to Christ, we need the Church. The Church *is* where we participate in Christ, and without the Church, we cannot have communion with Christ. Yes, we each have a personal relationship with Jesus for the simple fact that we are persons. But we too often interpret that phrase in an individualistic fashion as if to think, perhaps unconsciously, that my faith depends really and only on my life with Jesus.

This chapter has attempted to remove individualistic interpretations of our relationship with Jesus. The Church is the body that gives faith, that draws us into communion with Jesus, that brings about the unity of the faithful through her leadership, her communion, and her sacramental life. All of this serves the purpose of mediating—of making present— Christ to us. Thus, to have a personal relationship with Jesus, it must be through his body, which is the Church, because the Church is the place Jesus has chosen to reveal himself, to make himself known to us, and to draw us up into his life. The Church is where the life, death, and resurrection of Christ are always played out in all its members. In many, varied, mysterious, and secret ways Jesus is working his redemption in us through the life of the Church. We are all in Christ because we are all in the Church, and the Church, therefore, is always making his death and resurrection visible to the world. In short: the Church is the place of the sacramental worldview. It is where Christ works out his salvation in us through the sacramental life, through our communion, so that we can be a sacrament of Christ to the world.

This has many profound implications. For example, we see already that the sacraments do not merely feed us, but unite us to the broader and more universal mission of Jesus.

Yes, there is an individual character to the sacraments by virtue of the fact that they're always applied to individuals, but that is the secondary purpose of the sacraments. The primary purpose is for them to unite the whole Church to Christ and his mission. The sacramental life brings individuals outside of themselves and draws them into union with Christ, who offers his life as an oblation for the world. Thus, the sacraments and, more broadly, the Church, are a training ground for crucified love, whereby we pour out our lives for others that they may know the love of God as well. In short, the Church, her sacramental life, and her hierarchical structure all serve one purpose: to draw all the members into Christ and help them, in their own particular missions, to allow Christ to live out his redemption in and through them. Through them, Christ's redemption is made visible for the world to see, thus fulfilling the Church's role as the sacrament of salvation.

To open our hearts to the Church, to understand the Church more perfectly, and to prepare ourselves for the life of discipleship, it is important to look to the icon of discipleship: Mary. In Mary we see the perfection of the Church, the perfection of discipleship, and some key virtues to help us embrace the sacramental worldview and our stance in and toward the Church.

CHAPTER 6

The Marian Stance

WHEN I WAS IN SEMINARY, I struggled to pray the Rosary. I had a hard time in general with repetitive, rote prayers. I had difficulty seeing their importance. I often wondered, "Why should I pray these forms of prayer when there are higher forms such as contemplation and meditation?" Yet I did have a sense that I was missing something. So, on one of my seminary retreats, I decided to pray the Rosary every day. One day during the retreat, I read that Mary's heart was pierced so she could make her own experiences accessible to all of us in the Church. Suddenly, I had a realization about the Rosary. I finally understood that every time I said a Hail Mary, I wasn't so much doing repetitive prayer as I was asking Mary to give me a share in her experience of the mystery of the Rosary I was meditating on—to let me have her pure, immaculate vision of the mystery.

This experience ultimately gave me a different view of the Rosary and the role of Mary in the life of the Church. To me, Mary was no longer just the greatest of the saints but the perfection of the Church. In fact, not only is Mary the perfection of the Church, but she also has a real relationship with all the members of the Church. Because she carried Christ in her womb, and because the Church is the body of Christ, there is a real maternal connection between Mary and each one of us. Because of our connection with her through Christ, she shares her experiences of Christ with us so that we can know Christ more deeply and intimately.

Archetype of the Church

The above story helps us see what an important move it was for the Second Vatican Council to place the discussion of Mary in the last chapter of *Lumen Gentium*, Light to the Nations, the Dogmatic Constitution on the Church. This was of vital importance: the Council wanted to emphasize the role of Mary as the archetype of the Church. What does this mean?

To speak of Mary as the archetype of the Church means not only that the Church should imitate her virtues and perfections, but also that in Mary we find the full expression of what the Church is meant to be: "In the most Blessed Virgin the Church has already reached that perfection whereby she exists without spot or wrinkle."[1] In these words we see that Mary personifies, in a very concrete way, the perfection for which the Church strives. She gives the perfect response to Jesus in her *fiat* (her yes to God). She stands silently at the cross on Calvary. She is present in the Upper Room at

---

1. *Catechism of the Catholic Church*, no. 829.

Pentecost. In Mary, the Church finds her perfect response to the salvation of Jesus. Thus, not only is Mary the image of the Church, she is the Church perfected. Everything about Mary is not only instructive to us as Christians; it can form our attitude as we open our hearts to God.

This role of Mary goes further. As indicated in the seminary story, in a mysterious way we even participate in Mary. Because we are tainted by original sin, we are all sinners, incapable of giving a perfect "yes" to Jesus. But Mary has a perfect yes, and gives that yes to Christ on our behalf, thereby incorporating us into her "yes" with motherly care. Mary's answer is the answer of all humanity in search for God. She is also the Church's "yes"; that is, those who immerse themselves in the Church participate in her yes, thereby perfecting our imperfect and hesitant yes. We then, through the mystery of the Church, share in a special way in Mary's vision of the mysteries of Christ and have a relationship with her that is real and alive because she is alive, body and soul, in heaven. To be a Christian is, in a mysterious way, to have access to Mary, who allows us to see her Son perfectly through her.

To be a Christian is to be Marian, and to encounter the sacramental worldview means that we need to move away from a purely pragmatic and action-oriented attitude and develop the attitude of Mary. Of course, practical tools for the spiritual life and for Christian living are important. And activity in and of itself is not a bad thing. But as a Church we have lost the Marian attitude and have allowed ourselves to be overrun by activism, programming, and planning. This focus on constant doing creates a real poverty of heart, closing us off from the wellsprings of grace that come from a

Marian stance. A Church that acts but doesn't pray and plans but doesn't ponder is a Church more in the image of ourselves than the body of Christ. Since the Church consists of all baptized people in Christ, this means that, while the Holy Spirit ultimately and always directs the Church, the direction and attitude of the Church is also very much influenced by the direction and attitude of her members. A rediscovery of Mary's stance, therefore, is imperative. Discovering it forms us in the attitude we need for the Church's sacramental vision to take root in us. This Marian stance can be summarized in three words: receptivity, contemplation, and humility.

Marian Receptivity

The word "receptivity" is seldom viewed in a positive light these days. In a world where we are defined by what we achieve, doing is prioritized over being. This is highlighted simply in the question we often ask people when we first meet them: "What do you do for a living?" It's not a bad question to ask, but it's emblematic of the attitude of our historical moment. We define ourselves by what we do. We can't help it. It's in the roots of our being: you are what you do. What this attitude does, though, is emphasize doing over being, action over contemplation, giving over receiving. This attitude is a masculine approach, in which doing, fixing, and activism have become the primary mode of life. Furthermore, because of the overemphasis on doing, we underemphasize or even look down on receptivity. This, however, is a rebellion of our nature against a basic fact of being human: we are fundamentally and primarily receptive and dependent.

Receptivity is difficult to define succinctly because it is at the heart of the human experience. It means openness, contemplation, pondering. In the life of faith, receptivity means humble openness in one's heart to receive God. Receptivity has a lot in common with the idea of dependence. This is why Jesus exhorts us to become like children (see Mt 18:3). Infants depend totally on their parents in order to live. Everything they do requires the careful attention of their parents. And in that total dependence they bring much joy to their parents and everyone around them.

The embrace of dependence points to the need and desire to be receptive in a healthy fashion. To be receptive is the most human thing we can do, because it's how we are before God. We do not create ourselves; no one sustains himself or herself. Everything we have and are depends on God. Receptivity, built into our very being, is the most fundamental stance of humanity and it's embodied most perfectly in Mary. Mary is not only the perfection of the Church, she's also the pinnacle and perfection of humanity. In Mary we see how we are to be human, how we are to respond to God.

To be receptive requires several things. First, we must denounce the activism that overtakes our lives. By activism we mean the choice to constantly do before pondering and reflecting. It's a refusal to provide space and openness in our hearts for God to do his work in the world. If all we do is *do*, and we never learn to *be*—to get in touch with our fundamental need and desire for God—we will never be able to see him at work in all things. We will never be able to understand that grace really is mysteriously at work—not only in our own lives, but in the Church and in the world.

In order to overcome our tendency toward activism, we can look to the example of Mary, who had an eager anticipation to receive God into her life whenever God saw fit to make himself known to her. Second, we must cultivate both docility and quietness of heart. Only in docility and quietness can we hear the voice of God addressing our soul. Mary's receptivity is a humble, patient waiting to receive whatever God has in store for her. Even waiting is a constant *fiat* on the part of Mary. Such an attitude opens our heart to listen, to receive, and thereby to perceive the presence of God made manifest through the physical things of creation.

Naturally, however, we might struggle to see the value in receptivity. We often look down on this trait because it's considered weak and passive, and we often equate passivity with becoming a doormat. But this is not the Christian view of receptivity. Mary is always aware of God acting. She has an active receptivity because she always wills and desires to say yes to God whenever he wants to act. To embrace the Marian virtue of receptivity, then, we must ask for her help. And, more concretely, we must come to understand receptivity as both positive and essential to the human experience. Unfortunately, we in the West have become far too activistic. To slow down and learn to receive from God once again in and through Mary would provide a prophetic witness for the busy world in which we live.

One of the Church's greatest secrets is the value and primacy she places on femininity. We can discover this by looking at Mary. Based on what we've said above, this shows that there is something primary to our humanity—as males and females—that is feminine. To be human *is* to actively seek with an open and receptive heart the God who fulfills us. Thus, this feminine characteristic, which is also de facto a universal human characteristic, indicates a real treasure that needs to be rediscovered when discussing what it means to be human. This informs not only women, but even men, demonstrating that to be truly human, there is a requirement for docile receptivity from each of us. This is not only exemplified by Mary, but also by Jesus, who learned at the feet of Mary what it means to be human. Throughout the Gospels, when Jesus goes up the mountain to pray what does he do but receive from the Father? When the Church can take seriously this truly positive notion of receptivity, only then can the Church become herself. And one place the Church lives out this virtue of receptivity is in contemplation.

Marian Contemplation

Receptivity and contemplation go hand in hand. They do not happen in logical sequence; rather, they are an intertwined reality. Mary's receptivity is intertwined with her contemplation. Just as she encounters the Angel Gabriel and receives her mission from God, her first response is to ponder the meaning of the greeting (see Lk 1:29). Contemplation means that we are constantly alert, waiting for God to speak. And once God has acted, or perhaps is still silent, we ponder this in our heart. We ruminate over the words of Scripture, over the inspirations of prayer, and even over our dryness. We let the word seep into our hearts slowly, so the transformation of grace can take hold of us. This is Mary's attitude in the heart of the Church. She ponders the mysteries of God's actions, the mysteries of Christ's life, and keeps them in her heart for the sake of the whole Church. Through God's grace, she makes her experiences available to the whole Church, so that through her we can see Christ in an objective and pure manner. And in our own life of contemplation, we have access to these mysteries through Mary. Thus, we can always ask her, "Give me the vision of your Son," and she will respond.

The Marian attitude of contemplation and receptivity plays an important role in the Church's liturgy. Following the Second Vatican Council (though not inspired by it) the idea of active participation was misunderstood and applied in a twisted way. Participation in the Mass was reduced to a form of Western activism. People began to see liturgy as alive only insofar as more people were doing more things. But the idea of active participation is better understood through the lens of Mary. If we understand activity in a more receptive and contemplative mode, then we can see liturgical participation less as something we must do to make the liturgy alive and more as a place to be open to Christ working his salvation in us. Active receptivity simply means receiving what Jesus wants to offer us, namely, salvation. When receptivity and contemplation go hand in hand as in Mary, then liturgy very much becomes about what God does in us rather than about what we do for God.

Marian Humility

Mary's receptivity and contemplative attitude are rooted in the foundational attitude of humility. Her humility is the virtue whereby she acknowledges the truth of herself, of God, and of all reality. For all Christians humility is really a virtue that comes with faith. As we have established, faith is a gift, so in order to receive this gift according to God's terms and not our own, we must have humility. Mary's humility is the reason she is able to say yes to God completely: because she knows she is fully dependent on God; she knows that everything is a gift from him which requires her yes. Humility acknowledges that our dependence on God is the source of our freedom, and this is something Mary lives out perfectly.

One place where it is important for Christians to exercise this form of Marian humility is in respect to the Church's teaching office, the magisterium. Because she is Christ's body, and therefore belongs to Christ, the Church is by her nature the custodian of faith. She guards the parameters of the life of faith as given her by Christ through the magisterium, the pope, and the bishops in communion with him. By acting to guard the deposit of faith, the magisterium protects the image of the Church and helps direct us to ensure that the Church is constantly imaged after Mary. In other words: Christians participate in Mary's humility when they are humble toward the Church's teaching office because this teaching office mediates to us God's teachings given to us by Christ.

The Church's teaching and liturgical practice, then, are not simply rules made up by men to control Catholics. The teachings of the Church help guide us to enter into the life of Jesus. And the Church's liturgical practices, through sign and symbol, help communicate the grace of faith and thereby build up Christ's body. However, humility is needed on the part of all Christians to submit to Church authority and recognize that the hierarchy is not a creator of dogma and doctrine but rather a custodian of the deposit of faith. When protecting the teachings of the Church, the magisterium is acting out of a Marian form of humility. All of this helps ensure that the body of Christ will remain of one heart and mind, so that the one life of faith may be lived out in the lives of all the members of Christ's Church. If we recognize this, then we also recognize that the Church is not an obstacle to encountering Jesus but rather is the very place and means for encountering him.

Mary and the Sacramental Worldview

To develop a Marian stance is to develop the attitude necessary for the sacramental worldview. Mary is a concrete person: she is alive in heaven, body and soul. In her we perceive what the Church and disciple should be like. Through and in her, we see Christ more perfectly. Because she is full of grace, Mary is also a channel of the saving grace we need for eternal life. She is a sign, someone through whom we participate in Christ and experience his saving grace. This is sacramentality. If we want to embrace the sacramental worldview, we must embrace Mary: without her, we will continue in our activism and close our hearts to God.

How, then, can we cultivate this Marian stance? Receptivity, humility, and contemplation are not the world's values. In view of all we have to do in life, having these attitudes may seem impossible. Tranquility of heart, simple reflection, slowing down—none of these come naturally to us. Instead, we are overwhelmed by screens, noise, and distractions. Yet the Marian stance is vital for the Christian. And we can cultivate it through concrete actions.

To be more Marian, we can focus on God by waiting for him to speak. Concretely, this means that each day we must give time to God in prayer. Mary knew the work of God through the law and the prophets. Scripture is a privileged place to listen for God to speak to us. In prayer, we can take time to allow God to speak to us, especially by praying slowly over the Scriptures. However, praying is not only about serving our own needs. Of course, when we pray, something is at work for our own good. Prayer is an encounter with God and his love for us! But Mary has an openness of heart that protects against such attitudes as spiritual narcissism. She did not pray only for her own spiritual good and neglect thinking about others. When she prayed, she had a totally open heart toward God.

At the center of Mary's prayer and therefore our stance in her is that her prayer always holds things in her heart for the good of the whole Church. She holds the mysteries of Christ's life in her heart not for her own sake but out of charity and love for the Church. This means that when we go to pray, we must form ourselves according to the central secret of Mary: she wants to give us everything that is hers. Mary ponders the gifts of God's works in her life not for her own sake, ultimately, but to share with everyone all that is in her heart. In other words, the mysteries of God's actions in the life of Mary—including all the events surrounding her Son—are not for her to keep in her heart as a secret gift for herself. She gives them all away. And as Mother of the Church, she offers them to all the Christian faithful, so they may encounter and see her Son through her eyes. By entering into prayer and sharing the fruit of our prayer with others, we become sharers with Mary in bringing the grace of Christ to the whole world. Through prayer, we help the Church live out her mission as the sacrament of salvation in which the saving grace of Christ is made present and known to the whole world.

Entrusting our journey to Mary is the first and most important step in acquiring the Marian stance. Through the secret workings of God's grace, we begin to approach the world differently when we allow Mary to guide us. Her maternal care and affection help us see God anew. We begin to see Scripture as she sees it—as pointing us to an encounter with her Son. We begin to see the sacraments as gifts to be received and the starting point of Christian mission. Ultimately, we see the whole world as pointing us to an encounter with God. Although acquiring the whole Marian stance can seem daunting and even a little scary at first, we can rest assured that all we need to do is take the first step and God will do the rest.

To conclude this chapter, let's pray a simple prayer, trusting that the Lord will help us to acquire a Marian stance in our lives. Let us ask Mary to guide, protect, and help us to grow into seeing the world as it's meant to be seen.

> Mary, my mother and mother of the Church,
> Give me your heart to see as you see.
> Help me to encounter the mysteries of Christ's life
>   through your eyes.
> Help me to see the Church and the world through
>   your eyes.

Open to me the secret recesses of your heart so that I
    may know your Son.
Give me a heart like yours: receptive, always pondering,
    completely charitable.
Draw me close to your Son, and help me to find
    the truth that has been with me since Baptism:
I am a member of Christ's body and therefore I am
    in Christ.
Dearest Mother, pray for me.

PART THREE

Living the Sacramental Worldview

CHAPTER 7

Liturgy as Living Out Christ's Life

ONE OF THE MOST MEMORABLE books of literature I've ever read is *Brideshead Revisited* by Evelyn Waugh. The story revolves around a character named Charles Ryder, his time at Oxford, and his career as an artist. Charles is agnostic; he maybe believes that God exists, but he has little to no time for anything ritualistic. He sees the notion of sacraments, liturgies, ritual, as truly silly. Through his acquaintance with Sebastian Flyte at Oxford, Charles becomes familiar with all of Sebastian's family, including his father, Lord Marchmain, a convert to Catholicism who has ceased to practice his faith. Charles is present with the family when Lord Marchmain is on his deathbed and a priest is called to anoint him. Despite his own irritation and conviction that this hocus pocus is unnecessary, Charles has a sudden turn of heart. Suddenly, and clearly, a simple prayer for God to help Lord Marchmain comes upon him, and he prays this prayer sincerely. Lord

Marchmain makes the sign of the cross, indicating that he desires the sacrament of anointing, and the priest subsequently reconciles Lord Marchmain to Christ and his Church just before he dies. It is a powerful and dramatic scene (I highly recommend the book) through which Charles comes to a conversion around ritual, liturgy, and sacrament.

Charles has similar attitudes to so many people today who struggle to understand why God would require something like liturgy for participation in his life. Especially for people who are not Catholic, ritual is a difficult hurdle to overcome in order to understand the sacramental worldview. But it's a hurdle that must be jumped. While the sacramental worldview is about living all aspects of Christian life, liturgy is certainly at the center. In liturgy we participate in the different events of Jesus' life through liturgical feasts and seasons. We encounter his paschal mystery in the sacrifice of the Mass; we share in Jesus' praise of God in the Liturgy of the Hours; and we participate in the celebration of the sacraments. All these are deeply meaningful. Yet many persons have difficulty appreciating the centrality of liturgy. This attitude often arises out of hesitancy toward ritual.

Many see ritual as man-made, ossified, old, and boring—something that doesn't touch human experience. But a brief look at our own experience quickly proves that ritual is at the heart of how we act as human beings. Most of us love to celebrate birthdays and anniversaries, yearly events we commemorate in some ritual fashion, for instance with a cake or a nice dinner out. We love the pageantry of parades and the solemnity of graduations. Many of us have a morning ritual of exercise or quietly sipping our coffee while catching up on the news. Sporting events are great examples of ritual as well. Athletes have rituals they go through before each game, and the response and interaction of the crowd with the game is highly liturgical! Civic life also revolves around commemorations of political events and leaders. This is just a small sampling, but it doesn't take long for us to see that we are creatures of ritual.

Therefore, our resistance to ritual can be seen not so much as aversion to ritual in general as aversion to *religious* ritual specifically. In order to understand why this is so, it's helpful to recall the difficulties that modernism poses. Modernism denies that God can work in the world, which is why we doubt that God works through ritual. But the very reason the Church embraces ritual is because ritual is so human. God created us and knows how to reach us, so he works through the most human of things. We tend naturally to worshipful action because, in fact, we are created for worship, and ritual embraces our embodied, created nature to help direct our worship. Furthermore, worship is always a communal activity; it is never done in isolation. Worship is done for and on behalf of a community of believers to orient them toward God. Therefore, specific forms and laws around worship are introduced so we may all worship in the same manner.[1]

---

1. A fantastic book on this idea that we are created for worship is *Leisure: The Basis of Culture* by Joseph Pieper. Pieper explores how leisure is oriented to worship, which is fundamental to human beings, and it is upon this fact of our humanity that the Church's whole liturgical life is built.

Through her liturgical life, the Church embraces the centrality of ritual in human life. In the liturgy, God draws us into the mysteries of Christ's life in real and varying ways. These liturgical rituals touch place and time, matter and spirit—everything about our humanity. Through ritual signs and symbols, liturgy communicates specific ways we participate in the very life of Christ made present to us today. Liturgy, then, involves much that is indeed man made, but it's not for a man-made purpose. A simple example of this is the bread used in the Mass. By all accounts, bread is a man-made invention. No data tell us that God inspired humanity to invent bread. But, in the gift of the Eucharist, God takes this man-made object and lifts it up for a divine purpose, helping us to participate in God's very life. Indeed, why wouldn't God want to lift up the goods of creation like bread, wine, water, oil, incense, fabric, stone, and so on? The whole point of our redemption is that God draws all things to himself (see Jn 12:32). The use of these materials in liturgy foreshadows what God intends for creation at the end of time. Created things are lifted up to cooperate with God's saving action and made holy as a sign of what will happen at the end of time to everything God has created.

Entering Christ's Life

There is no better place to begin looking at liturgy than with the first sacrament we all receive, in which we are washed by water to be lifted up into a new life: Baptism. Baptism is the ritual entrance into the whole of the Christian life. But it's no mere symbolic ceremony. Rather, it's a ritual more profound and real: a participation in the saving death and resurrection of Jesus Christ. Recall how we talked about mystery in our first chapter. Baptism is the mystery by which we enter into the Christian life. It's God's secret plan, revealed in Christ and effected by him, and we have access to this saving reality through the ritual of Baptism, which Christ instituted. Baptism is a *real* participation in Jesus' death and resurrection through physical, sacramental signs. The signs are not the reality but the means by which we have access to the reality. In Baptism, water and our immersion into it communicate death and our being lifted out communicates a resurrection to new life. By means of the matter used in the sacraments—oil, water, words, bread, wine, etc.—God makes the saving reality present.

Unfortunately, the event of our Baptism is often seen as just a nice ceremony. Once it's over we can so easily think that nothing new has happened. But Baptism is not a one-time moment relegated to memory books with pictures and a baptismal candle to commemorate the occasion. Something new *has* happened, because Baptism grafts us onto the body of Christ, the Church. The Church is Jesus' living presence in the world and his body is made visible in each baptized believer. The Church, then, is the place where Christ continues to live out the mystery of his life, death, and resurrection, and each individual Christian embodies Christ's life in his or her body: "I have been crucified with Christ; yet I live, no longer I, but Christ lives in me; insofar as I now live in the flesh, I live by faith in the Son of God who has loved me and given himself up for me" (Gal 2:19–20). By faith Christ's life is lived in us and embodied in us. To be a Christian is to live the mystery of Christ in us—to be a sacrament. Baptism, then, brings real participation and unity with the mystery of Christ's life! The liturgy of Baptism is what initiates this sacramental way of life.

The moment we are baptized, we are immersed into the very life of Jesus. His life and ours become intertwined, and he begins, in a mysterious way, to carry out the saving work of his cross and resurrection in us. We are constantly *in Christ*, in the mysteries of the events of his whole life. This is possible because the Holy Spirit makes present to us the whole of Jesus' life so we can have access to the saving graces that come from his life, ministry, death, and resurrection. Because we have been baptized, what happened in the past is made present to us today.

To help deepen what we're talking about, let's stretch our minds a bit and recall some theology we've discussed already. We'll do this by reflecting on the phrase "Jesus Christ is the same yesterday, today, and forever" (Heb 13:8). This is to say that Jesus has a past, a present, and a future, and it's all the same. The Jesus who was present with the disciples is the same Jesus present to us today through his Church, and the same Jesus will come again at the end of time. Thus, it's inaccurate and risky to treat Jesus as a mere historical figure, a person of the past whom we simply imitate. This same danger is present when the Scriptures are seen in a purely historical context. By viewing them this way, we deprive them of the content of faith that they can communicate to us in a living and dynamic way right now. Yes, Jesus and the Bible have a history and a past and it's worth studying those things in order to understand them better. But we must never forget that Jesus is risen from the dead, and therefore he's alive, present, and active today.

The past, present, and future are all one in Christ, but this is hard to wrap our minds around because we so often see time in a sequential manner. We forget that because of the resurrection and the sending of the Holy Spirit, time itself has taken on a new form whereby the past is always made present so that we can participate in it. If we forget this, it becomes easy to look toward the past with longing and think, "My faith life would be so much better if I were in the presence of Jesus as the apostles were." Well intentioned though this thinking may be, it undermines Jesus' lordship and presence in our lives today. Not only that, such reasoning becomes a subtle form of modernism because it ignores the truth that Jesus makes himself really present to us today *through* the Church, especially in her sacramental and liturgical life. Thus, for example, when we read the Sermon on the Mount, we are with the disciples listening to Jesus: he is speaking those words to us today! Because of his lordship, Jesus is always present to us and to his Church; he makes the past events present to us today by the power of the Holy Spirit to draw us toward our eternal goal. If this were not so, then the resurrection would not be what we claim it to be, because the resurrection means that Jesus is alive in a new way. He is no longer present in just one particular place and history but now that he is alive and at the right hand of the Father, he is present to the whole Church by the power of the Holy Spirit.

Through the whole life of the Church, especially liturgy, Jesus gives us access to live out and participate in his death and resurrection in a real way, and this has all begun because we are baptized into Christ. Every time we go to Mass—where we are present at the sacramental representation of Jesus' sacrifice—we are uniting to his cross the cross lived out in our own life. With Jesus we offer our crosses to the Father, and we receive strength to continue to live that pattern so as to follow Jesus' way more closely. To be a Christian means to open our hearts to Jesus and say, "Draw me into your cross and resurrection." To say this to Jesus, we need places, words, and gestures for expressing this to him. This is why liturgy is so important: it is the place where we respond with the whole Church to Christ's invitation along his way. This is the heart of living the sacramental worldview and of living the liturgical rhythms and rituals of the Church.

Living Christ's Life throughout the Liturgical Year

As we've discussed, Jesus' activity in the Church is not bound by time; Jesus is always active. Yet, we know we are timebound creatures. So the Church, in her wisdom, gives us a pattern and rhythm by which to celebrate the chronological events of Jesus' life. What we call the liturgical calendar—the fixing of feasts and seasons for the entirety of the Church year—begins with what is good about creation. By instituting a liturgical year, the Church recognizes the goodness of the rhythms and cycles of the created world. Morning, day, and night, the seven-day week, the seasons of the year, and the year itself all play an important role in the Church's liturgical life. In other words: God makes himself known to us through the rhythms of the year in order to draw us to himself through them. In this section, we will take a look at how we are lifted up into the life of Christ throughout the liturgical year.

The liturgical life of the year is lived out through weeks and days. Sunday holds a special place in each week because on Sunday our entire week is lifted up into Christ's worship of the Father. Sunday is the day of the resurrection and on each Sunday we live the great victory of Christ over sin and death. Each Sunday enters that mystery in a real and substantial way. But the point here is not just to go to church every week to remember the good things Jesus did for us. These liturgical markers help us to participate in the particular graces of these actions. When we abstain from meat on Fridays and do penance, for instance, we are really participating in a mysterious way in the cross of Christ. When we go to Mass on Sunday, the gathered Church shares in Jesus' worship of the Father and in his victory, and we let our time and God's eternity connect. God uses simple things like the days of the week to manifest the eternal grace of our redemption.

Even the times of day play a role in the liturgical life of the Church. All time belongs to God and through the Church he wants to draw all of creation—every place and time—into his life. Priests, religious, and many laypeople pray the Liturgy of the Hours throughout the day. It is part of the official prayer of the Church, whereby the entirety of the day is sanctified and offered to God. Some people like to mark their day by praying the Angelus at morning, noon, and night, as yet another way to allow God to draw us to himself through every aspect of the day.

In addition to weeks, days, and hours, the Christian life is also marked by the liturgical seasons. Each season has particular celebrations to emphasize the different aspects of salvation history in which we participate. Each season and feast is a "today." In other words, through the seasons and liturgical celebrations, what happened in the past occurs *now* in our life today.

The liturgical year begins with Advent, a time in which we participate in the waiting of the Old Testament for the coming of the Savior, and a time which, more proximately, points to our waiting for the Savior to come again. Thus, throughout the season of Advent, we hear the prophets foretelling the coming of the Messiah while the Church also waits for his second coming. Advent is a penitential season because we are called to enter into this time to build up our expectation for God to come to us and save us. This is why Advent is about the two comings of Christ: his coming at the end of time and his coming in the flesh at Christmas.

The season of Christmas leads us to reflect on the fact that God has become flesh. The celebration of the Incarnation is the beginning of our redemption. But we don't just reflect on this abstractly. Because God took on our flesh, we are now lifted up, through the liturgy, into Jesus' sonship. Let's look at one example that clearly shows how we are present in mystery at the birth of Jesus. At the conclusion of the Christmas Masses, there is a solemn blessing, which says, "May the God of infinite goodness, who by the Incarnation of his Son has driven darkness from the world and by that glorious Birth has illumined this most holy day, drive far from you the darkness of vice and illumine your hearts with the light of virtue."[2] Notice how it mentions the past event, the Incarnation, and how that event illumines Christmas here and now? This is the liturgy's way of showing us how we are present to this event and how the event is made present to us today, thereby showing us that while God took on flesh definitively two thousand years ago, he continues to take on flesh today in his body, the Church. This is just one small way we participate mysteriously in the event of Christmas.

Later in the year, during Lent, we participate in Jesus' time in the desert. Just as Christ fasted and did penance in the desert, he draws us farther away from sin and deeper into the life of God. This is why many Christians take on penitential disciplines during Lent, even disciplines not mandated by the Church. It's a tangible way we can participate in what Christ did in the desert.

Lent finds its climax in Holy Week: the celebration of Jesus' triumphant entry into Jerusalem and his subsequent trial, death, and resurrection. Holy Week itself culminates in the Sacred Triduum, the three days of Jesus' passover from death to new life on Holy Thursday, Good Friday, Holy Saturday and Easter Sunday. The Triduum begins on Holy Thursday evening when we celebrate the institution of the Eucharist and the priesthood. One of the most stunning

---

2. *The Roman Missal*, "Blessings at the End of Mass and Prayers over the People." Third edition (Ottawa Canada: Concacan Inc., 2011) copyright Canadian Conference of Catholic Bishops, 652.

aspects of the Holy Thursday celebration happens at the time of the consecration. This moment highlights all we've been talking about in regard to participation. Usually, in the words that preface the consecration we hear, "On the night he was betrayed he took bread..." But Holy Thursday is the one day a year that we hear, "On the day before he was to suffer for our salvation and the salvation of all, *that is, today*, he took bread . . ."[3] (emphasis mine). Here the Church emphasizes the participatory aspect of the sacramental worldview that we have covered many times in this book already. On Holy Thursday, we are with Jesus in the Upper Room and on that day specifically we participate in the event of the institution of the Eucharist. In a mysterious way, we are really and truly present in that moment through sacramental signs.

The Triduum continues with Good Friday, the only day of the year we do not have a formal Mass. On this day, the Church asks us to fast and abstain from meat as a small way we can share in the sacrifice Christ offers for us. The Church really sees this as a time when Christ is being offered up and, as his body, the Church is being offered up with him as well. To offer ourselves is to participate in the cross, where, with Jesus, the whole Church offers herself *for* the world. Thus, it's a time for the Church to live out her mission in a very intense manner by interceding for the world, and so the Good Friday liturgy includes solemn prayers for all the world.

Finally, Holy Saturday is the highlight of the Christian calendar. The words of the Exultet sung at the beginning of

---

3. *The Roman Missal*, 288.

the Easter Vigil communicate the essence of this celebration. We hear repeated over and over the words, "This is the night." This is not just a warm recalling of past events and what Jesus did for us two thousand years ago. No, the Church's liturgy is calling us to see anew that this night on which we are present *is* the day of the resurrection. Today, Christ is raised from the dead. Today, we have been given new life and hope. Today, sin and death have been trampled upon. And because the past is made present in the liturgy of Holy Saturday, those who participate are powerfully drawn up into this victory themselves.

An entire book could be written, and many have been written, about the liturgical year and liturgical time. But we'll conclude this chapter by pointing to a concrete way we can allow our participation in these sacred mysteries throughout the Church year to deeply impact our soul: fasting and feasting.

Fasting is required for Catholics two days of the year: Ash Wednesday and Good Friday. But fasting can be done anytime throughout the year. Marking Fridays with fasting and other forms of penance is a great way to show that "today" Jesus died. The cross is remembered during our week and Fridays take on a more somber tone. Other ways to mark Fridays are by adding extra time for prayer and by removing normally distracting aspects from our life. In this way, Friday becomes a day on which we participate in the cross, allowing the cross to redeem small aspects of our life. We must remember that if we are participating in Christ, we aren't doing these things simply for our own sake, but for the salvation of the world. Thus, by carrying out these practices we say to Jesus, "I want to unite myself to your cross so that the world can know and have your salvation." Fasting and penance need not be a Friday-only endeavor, either. When scandals hit the Church and the world or when we want to intercede for a particularly urgent intention, fasting and penance are great ways to allow Jesus to work his grace through his body, the Church.

But fasting and penance are not the only hallmarks of the Christian life. Feasting is equally important. Feasting doesn't simply mean having great spreads of food on particular occasions, though these have their place and importance. Feasting goes deeper. It's really a celebration of the goodness of creation. Partaking of creation's various goods in abundance marks a particular day and helps us to see concretely that this day on which we are feasting is really important. Feasting educates us in our redemption. Thus, solemnities and feasts of the Church ought to be celebrated with greater honor and filled with food, friendship, and leisure. Easter and Christmas, Sundays, the various solemnities of the liturgical calendar: these are all days that are worth marking with feasting. For individuals in particular, feasting on the day of one's patron saint is a great way to celebrate. All this builds up a joyful hope and declares that creation is indeed good and worth lifting up into God's life. Thereby this helps us see the ritual life and rhythms of the Church as ultimate goods for us.

But we are also marked by the Church's most important liturgical celebration. The greatest liturgical celebration that the Church has is the Holy Mass, where Jesus makes himself present to us and draws us into his worship of the Father. Let's now turn to the Mass to see how we really and truly participate in Christ's life with this great celebration.

CHAPTER 8

The Holy Mass: Christ Glorifies the Father Through the Church

WHEN THIS BOOK WAS FIRST proposed, the possibility of a world pandemic was far from my mind. Yet this book took shape largely within the context of the Covid-19 pandemic, so observing the reactions of many Catholics when the churches were shut was enlightening. Many people expressed sentiments like, "I can't live without the weekly Eucharist!" or "I have to access the sacraments to grow in my faith and survive this difficult time." These reactions troubled my heart, and as I prayed about them I came to realize that many indicated a fundamental misunderstanding of the sacramental worldview.

What happened to make catechized Catholics think that they could become holy only by frequenting the sacraments as much as possible? After all, many of the saints received Communion only a handful of times a year. Unfortunately, the catechesis some Catholics have received about the Eucharist leads them to either downplay its reality or to believe they cannot survive a few months without it. This way of thinking speaks to a very individualistic view of the spiritual life, something Pope Francis calls spiritual "navel-gazing."[1] In this worldview, the sacraments are considered only in regard to the effect they have on *me*. We forget that the sacraments, while building us up in holiness and intimacy with Jesus, also lead us to charity—to thinking less of self and more of others. This universal view of the sacraments based on the unity of the Church is more in keeping with the sacramental worldview. We receive the sacraments for our own sake, yes, but primarily to build us up for mission: to go and bring Christ to the whole world.

It is around this mission that the Mass is centered. The Mass lifts us up and allows us to participate in Christ's central act of worship of his Father: the paschal mystery. It is in the Mass that the Church is mysteriously elevated into this act of perfect worship. The Mass, then, is the greatest gift: it is there that we are sacrificed, die, and are raised up with Christ anew. And it is in the context of the Mass that we receive the gift of the Eucharist, his sacramental presence, so as to become more and more like him. When we go to Mass, then, we do not go so much to worship our own behalf as to be lifted up and participate in Christ's worship. This is why the Marian ideals of receptivity, contemplation, and humility that we mentioned in Chapter 6 are so important: they help

---

1. "Pope addresses the 'illnesses' of the Diocese of Rome," Vatican News, May 15, 2018, https://www.vaticannews.va/en/pope/news/ 2018-05/pope-francis-diocese-rome.html.

us become docile to being lifted up into Christ's action and allow him to form and mold us more and more into being the sacrament of his presence to the world.

If the Mass is the greatest form of participation in the life of God, then it becomes apparent that this is essential for the sacramental worldview. It is our means of participation, it is a ritual action that makes salvation present, and it reveals Christ in the most perfect way possible through the gift of the Eucharist. In a way, we could say that the Mass is the lens through which the sacramental worldview becomes most clear. Thus, it's important to walk through the different parts of the Mass not just to say what they are, but to see how we are lifted up to participate in Christ's worship. For some, this may be a bit of a review, but for others it may be new. The Mass is the sacrament of Christ's worship, and it is therefore essential for us to take a brief look at the parts of the Mass.

The Introductory Rites

The Mass begins with the priest stating a fact: "In the name of the Father, and of the Son, and of the Holy Spirit." The Church responds with "Amen," thus saying it's true. This sign of the cross with the invocation of the Trinity sets the tone for the entire liturgy. The sign of the cross at the beginning of Mass is not just a meaningless gesture: it means we are now *in* God's presence, we are dwelling in the Trinity. The entire Mass is a time of being lifted up into the communion of God. It is the most perfect form of participating in the life of God.

Then in the penitential rite we individually recall our sins. To allow Christ's redemption to take hold of us, we need to acknowledge our sins, so that the very action that frees us from sin—his death and resurrection—can take effect in us. In the Collect, the opening prayer, the priest says, "Let us pray." The "us" is the "we" of the Church. The priest's prayer is the prayer of the whole Church in Christ. In this moment, we are invited into Christ's prayer; through his prayer we are being lifted up into the presence of the Father. We are addressing the Father, asking him to make effective in our lives the saving mystery of his Son that we are about to celebrate. The whole point of the Introductory Rites is to aid us in this act of participating in Christ's worship and open our hearts to receive his word.

The Liturgy of the Word

The Liturgy of the Word has always been an integral part of the liturgy. Through the Acts of the Apostles we often hear about the role of the Scriptures in the early Church. The Gospels and Epistles, or letters, were written with the explicit purpose of being read out loud at the liturgies of the Church. Scripture, then, plays a vital role in the Mass. But Scripture is not just a message or reminder of what once happened in the history of salvation. Scripture is the means by which Christ, the Word of God, speaks to the Church today through human words. The whole of salvation history is made present in the Mass, and the Liturgy of the Word vocalizes this pattern of salvation history. Thus, in the first reading, we often hear from Israel's history in the Old Testament, which is meant to prefigure and point toward the story of the Church, the New Israel. This is why on Sundays and solemnities the first reading is always related to the Gospel and helps us interpret and understand the Gospel so we can hear God speaking to us today.

The whole Church responds to the first reading and the word received with the psalm. The Scriptures reveal God's Word to the Church, so there is no better way to respond to God than through his own revealed word in Scripture. The second Sunday reading doesn't usually follow a particular theme of that Mass' readings because it often has its own cycle. Nevertheless, though the epistles are letters addressed to a particular people in a particular time and place in the history of the Church, these too are always God addressing us today. Thus, for example, when Saint Paul exhorts the Corinthians to unity, he is exhorting all of us. The teachings of the apostles through their epistles have an active, living voice and an enduring value.

The Liturgy of the Word culminates in the Gospel, the moment in which Christ speaks in a definitive manner. Everything we've done thus far in the Mass leads up to this point. When we hear the Gospel, it's important to remember that we are not just listening to words being read. We are present in mystery at the real scene being proclaimed. If it's the Sermon on the Mount, for example, we are mysteriously there, hearing Jesus speak to us through the sacramental sign of the Scriptures. Christ is addressing us directly and drawing us into that particular mystery, inviting the Church to conform herself more and more to his way and his path. The entirety of the Liturgy of the Word, therefore, is not some add-on or unnecessary part of the liturgy. It's essential.

As creatures we often receive communications through words spoken and read. God respects this creaturely reality and wants to address every aspect of our being. Scripture and the preaching of the clergy are fundamental ways by which God mediates his presence to us. Yet God also wants to draw us even more deeply into his life and into more intimate communion with him. In other words, he doesn't just want to speak to us, he wants to dwell in us. And this dwelling is not just a spiritual reality: he wants to dwell in our whole humanity, body and soul, individually and as a singular body, as the Church. This is why the Mass culminates in the Eucharist: it's the means by which God offers himself to the whole Church in so total a fashion that he dwells within each of us deeply and intimately in body and soul and draws us into a deeper communion with the whole body of Christ.

The Liturgy of the Eucharist

The pattern of the fulfillment of the old in the new that we find in the Liturgy of the Word continues in the Liturgy of the Eucharist. The priest's prayer of blessing over the bread and wine comes from the Jewish Passover meal. The gifts of bread and wine that he blesses symbolize our work and entire lives as lived during the preceding week being lifted up to God to be transformed and renewed by his Son. God takes what is natural in these gifts and uses them to make something supernatural. But before we delve into the meaning of the consecration, let's review something we've already discussed.

Let's recall that the Mass is a real participation in Christ's worship of the Father. What Christ does on the cross is made present on earth each time Mass is celebrated. During the Mass, Jesus' one sacrifice is not merely remembered but is made present to us in sacramental form. In other words, God uses the rituals of the liturgy to make the death and resurrection of Jesus really present to us today. Thus, at Mass we are at Jesus' death, descent into hell, resurrection, and ascension—all at the same time. Going to Mass, therefore, is no mindless ritual. At Mass we are present to realities that transform and save us. Mass actually makes Christ's Body sacramentally present here in time and space as we are lifted up into that one eternal sacrifice by which we are saved. Because we are in Christ as the Church, we are in him in the paschal mystery made present in the words of consecration.

The priest's words at the consecration effect what they signify. This is a technical phrase meaning that when the words are said over the bread and wine, these are really and substantially changed into the Body and Blood of Jesus. Thus, when the priest says, "This is my body, given up for you," he is not only repeating the words of Jesus on the night of the Last Supper. Rather, this is an action of Jesus in which the priest participates. When the priest says the words "this is my body given up for you" and "this is my blood poured out for you," it is Jesus performing the action of consecration through the priest. With these words, Jesus also tells us something about the cross: it is not a pointless suffering; it is "for us." When we attend Mass and hear these words, we are mysteriously present at Calvary where Christ gives his body and blood for us so that we might have new life in him.

When we understand what is truly happening at the consecration it becomes clear why we kneel at this moment of the

Mass. We kneel because Jesus himself becomes sacramentally present to us. His Presence is really and truly in our midst. In this most solemn act, the Son of God offers his body for the life of the world so that we, his body, may be raised to new life in him. Our kneeling is the whole Church's act of adoration of this great gift.

As if this isn't astounding enough, the mystery goes even further. Through the Mass, Christ is not only made present to us. Because the Mass is Christ's offering of his body for the life of the world and because the Church *is* his body, this means that we are mysteriously united to him in his paschal mystery. This even happens when we are not physically present at the Mass! This is so simply because every Mass is a work of the whole Church, Christ's body, offering itself to the Father. This is signified by the fact that at every Mass we pray not only for the people present, but for all the Church.

At the reception of the Eucharist, God's communication to us, drawing us into his life, takes its most intimate form. Jesus' sacrifice on the cross gains its greatest effectiveness when we receive his Body made present sacramentally at the Mass. Christ, risen from the dead, is really and truly present in the Eucharist in his Body, Blood, Soul, and Divinity. But by receiving this gift we are not gnawing on the flesh of Christ. This is a *sacramental presence*. In other words, the Eucharist makes Christ really, truly, and substantially present—it is the whole Christ present—but his presence is mediated through the appearances of bread and wine.

By lifting up the Church into his sacrifice, Christ draws the whole Church into his life. By giving us his Body to eat and his Blood to drink in the Eucharist, Jesus helps conform us more to his body, the Church. We become little Christs for the world, not just as individuals but in service to a greater good. Yes, the Eucharist brings about our own sanctity, but it also brings about the Church's unity and communion. By receiving Communion, we communicate that we are in communion with the Church, Christ's body on earth. Through the Eucharist, Christ dwells not only in each of us but in the whole Church.

With this in mind, it's easier to understand why we should not receive the Eucharist when in a state of mortal sin, or living a public or private life contrary to Jesus' teachings. To receive the Eucharist in this state is to say, "Even though I'm not in communion with Christ and his Church through my way of life, I'm still going to receive the Communion that binds me to him." For this reason, sacramental confession is vital for someone who has fallen into serious sin.[2]

Of course, while the Eucharist unites the entire Church, we experience an individual effect too. In the Liturgy of the Word, God communicates his word to his Church through Scripture, while in the Eucharist God addresses us through his Word in sacrament. When we receive Communion—the fruit of Jesus' paschal mystery—Christ addresses us no longer through a spoken word but with his very presence in our soul

---

2. It may be that you have a great fear of confession and are afraid of being judged by the priest. But confession is not where Christ condemns us. Rather, it's where we participate in a particular way in his cross and resurrection. When we confess our sins, Christ lifts them up to the cross through the sacrament, thereby redeeming us from their hold over our life, bringing us back into communion with him.

and body. The Eucharist is a sign to us that God wants to redeem the whole of us and leave no part of us untouched or resistant to his love. Words fail to convey this kind of intimacy. It prefigures heaven and shows us the overwhelming love God has for us, that he would deign to dwell in us, body and soul, and have us dwell in him. The Eucharist is such a great gift, the foretaste of heaven!

Concluding Rites

Finally, after receiving the Eucharist we are dismissed from Mass. While the Mass is important as the culmination of our life of participation in Christ, we need to remember that this is not the only important moment in our day. The purpose of the sacramental life, whether the particular sacraments or the larger sacramental vision, is to spur us on to charity, to bring Christ's love to the world. For the laity specifically, the conclusion of Mass means we become a sort of tabernacle of Christ's presence to the world.

One of the most ignored teachings of the Second Vatican Council is the secular vocation of the laity. Unfortunately, at least in North America, we've clericalized the laity, thinking they are meant to live out their vocation by doing things in and for the Church. Instead, the Church is meant to be the springboard for the laity to bring Christ into all aspects of daily living, whether it be with family and friends, in activities, or at the workplace. When all we do is worry about what positions we hold in the parish, what tasks we are given, or what sort of prominence we may receive, then we have our focus in the wrong place. Rather, when we come to Mass, when we are in the parish, it is the place where we should *be*, rather than *do*, because liturgy, at its heart, is about being. Obviously, the clergy need the cooperation of the laity for the functioning of the parish, but in reality the laity's primary focus, mission, and energy should be devoted to their secular vocation.

The end of Mass ushers in the rest of the week. By being dismissed, the laity attending Mass are now sent on mission. Through their friendships, work, families, hobbies, they have contact with the world and bring Christ's presence into it. They are always members of the Church, always participating in the life of Christ—and Christ's life was lived to bring salvation and peace to a broken world. Thus, by being members of the Church, the laity are sent out to evangelize and be missionaries of God's love to a world desperately in need of it. This is an aspect of participation that radiates from the Mass: its effects ought to be a cruciform outpouring of love for a world that has fallen away from God. This is the duty and dignity of the lay vocation.

Mass: the Source of Mission

At the heart of the Mass is a real participation in Christ's saving mysteries that take effect in our lives. This effect then motivates us and fills us with the life of Jesus, which we always participate in even when we aren't able to go to Mass. At the heart of the sacramental worldview is the reality that we are baptized *into* Christ, not just on Sundays but every day. Our Baptism never leaves us. It's the means by which we are attached to Christ at all times. The sacramental worldview of participation in Christ enables us to see that even if we are unable to frequent the Eucharist for some reason, it doesn't mean that God's grace is not at work. It always is! Though we may not be able to receive Jesus intimately in the Eucharist, we can always have the intimacy of being in Christ through our Baptism. We must remember that, except in the case of serious sin, grace does not leave us. Grace, the life of Jesus given to us, is always at work. Therefore, we always have access to that life because we are really in him. Because we are in Christ by virtue of our Baptism, he is never far away. Jesus is always nearer to us than we are to ourselves.

Knowledge of always being in Christ helps protect us from treating the sacraments as magical objects or talismans. Participation is a two-way street: Christ offers us the gift of his life, but we need to respond with our yes to him. This participatory view guards us from having a magical view of the sacraments, expressed when we tend to see the repeatable sacraments as the only means to grace. By rediscovering the value of our Baptism, we come to see that every sacrament is a particular gift from God to draw us into his life and help perfect the fundamental baptismal grace. All this is meant to lead us to mission: to carrying the good news of salvation to the whole world. Every sacrament is at the service of mission.

With mission comes a responsibility on our part. Because we are Christians, we bear the responsibility of being a sign of Christ and must be careful that we do not become an anti-sign that contradicts the Christian message. When we fail to live the sacramental worldview, we support the view of those who doubt the efficaciousness of the sacraments. They say,

"See, this is nothing but empty ritual. It obviously has no real impact because it hasn't changed the hearts of the people who go to Mass." We must allow Christ to challenge us and spur us on to greater Christian love, so that we can show the world that Christ is alive and that his Church is the sacrament of salvation where life is found.

Liturgy ought never to create in us a spiritual narcissism that says, "What's in it for me?" This attitude undermines the very gifts we receive. Rather, when we participate in the saving mysteries of Christ, they ought to effect a real—though often slow—transformation of our hearts that impels us to spend ourselves for others. When this happens, our lives become proof that liturgy and ritual give life. But we need to grow spiritually to see the Mass, and all the seven sacraments, as aids drawing us out of ourselves and into mission in the world. This means that the Mass is not just something for me, but rather it is something that conforms me to Christ. This conformation takes place so that I may give my life away so that others may live. This is the heart of the Christian life, and it is toward this that the Mass, all the sacraments, and the whole sacramental structure of the Christian life is oriented. In order to effect this spiritual growth, we must constantly renew and deepen our relationship with Jesus so as to be open to conforming our lives to his every day. We open ourselves to this renewing love every time we converse with the Lord in prayer.

CHAPTER 9

The Mystery of Christian Prayer

I OFTEN ASK OTHER CATHOLICS, "How's your prayer life?" This gives them an opportunity to answer honestly and often without any shame. Some may hang their head and say, "I don't have much of a prayer life lately, father." Others will say something to the effect of, "Well, I make sure I say my prayers every night." Still others will confess to their daily Rosary and devotions, some to the reading of Scripture, and others to adoration, meditation, and a life of deep prayer.

My reason for asking Catholics this question is because through asking it I've come to realize one thing: a lot of Catholics do not know how to pray. This is not the fault of many. It just so happens that no one taught them what to do. But prayer is of essence to the Christian life because it is the means by which we grow in our personal relationship with Jesus and the life of discipleship we are trying to live. The Christian prays, and prays profoundly, not so much because we have to become advanced mystics. Rather, we pray because prayer was at the heart of Jesus' life and ministry.

The Gospels tell us just how often Jesus would pray. Many times, after an intense period of ministry, he would go up a mountain to pray in order to enter into communion with his Father. The disciples saw Jesus in prayer so often that they asked him to teach them how to pray. They saw something about Jesus' prayer that they wanted to imitate. In the Gospel of Matthew, Jesus says, "When you pray . . ." (6:5). He makes it clear that a Christian is expected to pray. He doesn't say, "If you choose to pray"—he presumes it will happen.

Prayer is where Christ speaks to us personally and intimately and builds up our communion with him so that the communion of the Church can grow. Without prayer, we cannot live the Christian life. The life of grace, the life of the sacraments, and the life of the Church are all possible only if we internalize and accept them with our whole heart through prayer. Personal prayer is the place where our love for God is deepened. If Jesus, who knew no sin, needed prayer for his mission, imagine just how much more we—great sinners that we are—need prayer.

When you think of Jesus at prayer, and then when you look at yourself in prayer, it's sometimes all too easy to see the disparity between your prayer and the prayer of Jesus. You may say your Rosary, your night prayers, perhaps read a little Scripture or a small devotional book, and pray for and with your family. But there are times where you may have no idea how to go beyond this. In view of Jesus' habits of prayer and the lives of the saints who experienced such intimacy with God, it's easy to feel stuck in a very basic pattern of prayer and have no idea how to grow.

The focus of this chapter is to help you to enter more deeply into prayer. Hopefully it's clear by now that everything we do as Christians we do in Christ. The sacramental worldview imbues in us a vision of the Christian faith that allows us to see the world through the eyes of Christ. Since all our activity is done in him, this is true of our prayer life as well. In fact, it's *especially* true of prayer.

Taking the principles of the sacramental worldview as a starting point, we can already see how alive and dynamic prayer is meant to be. Christ draws us into his prayer with the Father, and the Holy Spirit is the main actor in our life of prayer. But how can we contemplate God through the Scriptures, the circumstances of life, in our devotions and vocal prayers? The sacramental worldview sees prayer as dealing with the concrete stuff of life and drawing it into Jesus' life. All of life is the stuff around which prayer often grows.

What Is Christian Prayer?

So often, we would love to have a simple guide explaining the five steps to take for a perfect prayer life. We all like things to be measured and quantified, and prayer is no exception. These temptations are particularly present when we are attempting to establish a habit of prayer. They also happen whenever we say, "I don't feel anything in prayer" or, "I don't get anything out of it." As well intentioned as these phrases can be, they often point to a misunderstanding of prayer. We may be begging for a system, a five-step guide, or to "get something out of it." But if one reads the lives of the saints, one quickly sees how hesitant they are to present a system of prayer. Prayer is not a program toward self-actualization or something we do simply for personal gain: prayer is a relationship of love.

If prayer is a relationship of love, then we must shake off our tendency toward a pragmatic or utilitarian approach to prayer. If, for example, we are seeking to achieve the heights of Christian prayer for our own sake, as well intentioned as that may be, we are forgetting that prayer is about charity and loving God for his own sake. Nor can our prayer be measurable in its results. We are a mystery to ourselves, and God is the infinite mystery. Our desire for measurable or immediately perceptible results in prayer comes from our fallenness, because in it, we are attempting to bring God down to our level. Instead, when prayer is rooted in love, it cares not for measuring nor for personal gain but rather for simply being in the presence of the beloved.

It's important to state these reasons against the pragmatic mindset, because that mindset undermines the sacramental vision of reality. Instead of waiting to receive God, opening one's heart in wonder toward him through his creation, a pragmatic approach to prayer attempts to force God: it is about pride rather than humility. On the other hand, the sacramental worldview requires patient and humble waiting, openness of mind and heart, and a deep, abiding recognition that Christ is at work. Only when we can begin to attune our hearts to these virtues will the sacramental worldview infuse our life of prayer.

What is prayer, then, if it's not a pragmatic, measurable process? Remember how faith is a sharing in Jesus' vision of reality? And not just a sharing of Jesus' vision of creation but also his vision of the Father and immersion into the life of the Trinity? If faith means sharing in Jesus' vision, then we also share in everything else: Jesus' actions, his affections, his will, everything. Prayer, then, is nothing more than sharing in Jesus' deep union with the Father. When we pray, we talk to the Father in and through the Heart of Jesus by the power of the Holy Spirit. More than just a conversation, it's an immersion of our whole life and being into the life of God. Yes, prayer involves speaking and listening to God, but it goes even deeper—to pray is to enter into God's presence. Because God enters our humanity in Christ, so too in Christ our humanity is lifted up into the life of God. Prayer is the privileged place in which we begin to encounter the very life of God through Christ.

Now, some of us might read this and think that, while it's inspiring, we doubt that it's possible. We find it hard to want to pray; we are often distracted; we have no time; the duties of family life make it difficult to find silence. These are all real obstacles that can't be ignored. But these obstacles can also become excuses that we too easily yield to, preventing any real progress in the spiritual life. When we do not find the time to pray, allowing real obstacles to remain obstacles, we remove something essential from human life. To pray is to say to God, "I need you; without you I would not exist, I cannot live." By praying, we are making an act of total dependence on God, who thereby invites us into his life.

When we pray, we bring all aspects of our lives to God: our difficulties, distractions, hesitations—everything. Prayer throws our whole life into God's life and allows God to draw us into his very heart. It may be incredibly hard for us to do this and to trust God. We fear to bring our sins and attachments to God. But if we take the cross seriously, sin is not an ultimate barrier to God. Sin is what Christ wants to take up into himself through the cross. Therefore, our personal sins and attachments are taken up and transformed by Christ, and thus we shouldn't fear bringing them to God in prayer. One could even say that to some extent our sins are the means by which we begin to enter into deeper communion with God.

Thus, prayer has a purifying purpose. It becomes a place where we are honest with God. To some extent, God challenges us in prayer and asks us for something more. But it's not an accusation—accusation comes from the accuser, the devil, and not from God. Prayer is always an invitation of love. As Saint Paul tells us, "Where sin abounds, grace abounds all the more" (see Rom 5:20). Prayer is the crucible of love where we are really and truly united with Christ on his cross.

We've discussed the generic sense and purpose of prayer. But it's also important to remember the sacramental theme of this book in relation to prayer. Because we are embodied, sacramental creatures, we need something sensible to aid and direct us in our prayer: for example, words, beads, incense, images. When we forget this, we often enter into prayer expecting a sort of blank slate or imageless experience. Rather, using aids in prayer is not opposed to contemplative prayer; these aids are the very means to union with God. In the rest of this chapter, we'll explore some forms of prayer that can help us participate in the life of Christ.

Spoken Prayer

The majority of us are most familiar with spoken prayer. Whether it's the Rosary, novenas, the Divine Mercy Chaplet, or Liturgy of the Hours, we are all accustomed to spoken prayer. This form of prayer finds its foundation in Jesus' teaching of the "Our Father." By giving his disciples this prayer, Jesus highlights the importance of spoken prayer in the Christian life. Formal spoken prayers can be repetitive and consoling—a rock to lean on, especially when we don't feel like praying. Not intended as a sort of incantation, these prayers are meant to mark each moment of our lives by acknowledging God's presence and action.

In the Garden of Gethsemane, Jesus also models for us a more informal spoken prayer when he speaks directly to the Father. Spoken prayers like this can be used during set prayer times as well as throughout our day. We may be carrying out a task and suddenly exclaim, "Jesus, help me" or "Jesus, have mercy on that person's soul." Small outbursts of spoken prayer are attempts in a particular moment and place to bind our intentions to the heart of God—to bring Christ's kingship into this particular situation and moment. To speak formally or informally in prayer, therefore, is essential to Christian prayer because it was essential in Jesus' prayer.

Praying with Scripture

Spoken prayer is helpful to our prayer lives, but it can't stop there. Prayer is a conversation and immersion into the very life of God. This requires a certain tuning in to the greater reality of God. This prayerful tuning in can only happen when we also listen to God. In fact, listening is more important than speaking. Spoken prayers are meant to lead us into a deeper relationship with God so that we may listen to God speaking to us. And one of the best places to learn to listen to God is Sacred Scripture.

God speaks to us in a sacramental fashion, using human words to communicate with us and draw us into his life. It is for this reason that he set up Scripture as a privileged place to listen to him. The Scriptures are not a collection of antiquated texts that only tell us about past events. The Bible is not primarily a history textbook. Scripture, rather, is the Word of God—Jesus Christ—given to us through human words. Because the words of Scripture are God speaking to us today, they always have a freshness and newness when we approach them, making them inexhaustible.

Scripture, then, is a great tool for helping us grow in our communion with God. Here, God really speaks to us by mediating himself to us through the words of Scripture. One particular practice of prayer with Scripture in which God speaks to us is known as *Lectio Divina*. A Latin phrase, lectio divina is literally translated as "divine reading," which can be understood in two senses. First, it's a divine reading in that we read the scriptural text through God's vision of things. But it's also a divine reading of ourselves, of our souls, of the Church. Thus, lectio divina is also a way for God to read us!

The practice usually focuses on a small passage, about three to five verses, and follows four steps. First, you read the passage a few times, slowly. Then you meditate on a word or phrase that struck you in the reading. Following this, you spend time praying to God, thanking him for speaking to you, and speaking words of praise in gratitude. Finally, there is contemplation. Here it is important to just practice being in the presence of the God who has spoken to you and drawn you more deeply into his life. This is where silence enters, and you simply delight in the fact that you have been and are in the presence of God. Here we begin to see hints of what heaven is like, because heaven is nothing more than being in God's presence. We could even say that this final step of contemplation begins to bring heaven to earth as we encounter God's presence and delight in it here and now. Lectio divina is a powerful tool whereby God uses something essential to our humanity—words—to draw us into a deeper encounter with him through the words of Scripture.

Lectio divina is but one of many resources we can use when engaging with Scripture in a prayerful fashion. For example, Saint Ignatius, in both his spiritual exercises and in forms of meditation, offers imaginative prayer as a great method of using Scripture. The key is that Scripture gives us something we can focus on through which God reveals himself, because we often need this when attempting to begin or advance in a regular prayer life. There is no better tool than Scripture!

The Examen

It is common for Catholics to want to make an examination of conscience. In fact, we do this in a brief form whenever we are at Mass. But the examen is a daily practice that does something more than simply acknowledge our faults. It has many similar principles to lectio divina. But instead of using Scripture as the means through which we encounter God, the examen uses our life and conscience to see his presence.

The examen begins by invoking the Holy Spirit, asking for his guidance and help, and placing yourself in the presence of Christ, who is our guide and help. In fact, the examen is really nothing more than a reflection on your day through the eyes of Jesus. You review the day with Jesus, recognizing where you've seen him, or perhaps you recognize his presence for the first time during the examen. You give thanks for those places where you've encountered him. You acknowledge your failures in thought, word, and action, and you ask for forgiveness. As an attempt to avoid falling into the same patterns again, you make a resolution for the next day. It ought to be a single, manageable, and concrete solution that you can easily act upon. Then, you close with a prayer such as the Glory Be.

What's especially helpful about this prayer is the fact that we are praying it in Christ. This helps us to not fear our sin and failures when we have to look at them. Sin and failure so often leave us without hope because we look at them without Christ. The examen helps us to remember that Christ is with us always and that even when we fail to grow closer to him, he uses that moment to imbue us with his grace so he can transform us. Thus, when we look at our failures, that doesn't build a sort of guilt complex, but rather builds up hope that, because we are in Christ, we have a God who is always seeking to heal, transform, and renew us and who never wants to abandon us.

The examen is a great practice to do every night. It can take from five minutes to as long as one needs or desires. An especially helpful tool in the examen is to journal the key events and actions that emerge from our time of prayer. The reason for this is simple: the fruit of prayer is discernible but, as we said above, not measurable. Over time, in our prayer we can begin to see patterns and growth that help us to recognize God's action as fruitful, though often done in secret. Looking at things this way builds up a general hope in our lives, and we realize that the small disturbances of life probably aren't such a big deal as we tend to make them, because God really is at work to draw us into his life forever.

Contemplation

Contemplation is the height of Christian prayer because it's the one form that involves us the least. Contemplation is a pure grace. In it, God chooses to lift us up into his life in an experientially profound way that is both completely familiar and completely foreign. Contemplation is nothing else than allowing God to draw us into his heart, and seeing God as he really is, even if the experience seems at times to be fleeting and grasping.

Contemplative prayer is thus also the most difficult topic to discuss. Because it's a pure grace and gift from God to be in his life in an ever deeper way, this implies that there is no real method that can guarantee we will receive this grace. We cannot demand a gift; it has to be given freely. What we are asked to do—through the methods of prayer mentioned as well as countless others—is to prepare our heart for this grace. In this life contemplation is the closest gift we can receive to what heaven will be like. It means to be in the heart of God, to see the world through his eyes, to remove ourselves from self so completely so that God can permeate every aspect of us. Contemplation, then, is really the height and goal of the Christian life.

To enter into contemplation we must have that Marian stance we spoke of, by which we ponder the mysteries of God. This means that we need a quality of listening and receptivity that builds up our desire for God. This in and of itself is an important undertaking. Working on attitudes and times for silence is essential, and by doing so, we will see these as the most human moments we have, so we'll want to have more of them. These moments are the most human because they are the most Marian: in both Mary and Jesus we see the centrality of silence in prayer, and this therefore reveals that in silence there is something central to being human. This can only be discovered through an actual practice of silence so as to give the heart space for God to speak. It is here that our desire for God increases, and God, who loves us and wants to lavish us with his love, responds to our desire with his very self, giving us the grace of contemplation.

However, growing in silence, receptivity, and listening doesn't mean removing from our prayer such aids as Scripture, the Rosary, or the experiences of our life. No. These are the very means to contemplation: through them, by building up our faith, we begin to discern the presence of God as really and truly active. Contemplation is simply resting in God's presence, which is revealed through our life, our prayer, our meditations, our growth, etc. Contemplation, then, is the culmination of all we do and say through which God reveals himself and through which we simply dwell joyfully and peacefully in his presence.

What is beautiful about contemplation in the Christian tradition is that it is not an escape into pure spiritualism, a way to ignore or even denigrate the body. Rather, for the Christian contemplative prayer is where God meets us as we are, body and soul. It's a prayer that involves the whole person. Thus, it's a very intimate way in which God uses the stuff of creation—in this case, our very bodies—in order to draw us into an encounter with him. Christian contemplative prayer is God's way of affirming what he's created in us and saying that our whole self really is meant to be with him.

Total Dependence on God

Our discussion about prayer has avoided offering tips for a better prayer life. This is on purpose. As we've stated, prayer is not a system to be figured out. To do so would be to put ourselves above God. Rather, prayer is about developing an attitude of humility that recognizes, at the core of our being, that we are creatures in need of our Creator. We recognize deep within ourselves a dependence on the One who created us, and prayer is our expression of that dependence: "God, I need you; I cannot live without you; be in my life."

Christian prayer is an intensification of this fundamental human phenomenon. Our dependence is now lifted up into the life of the Son of God, who descended into our world and took on human flesh. This act of humility by the Son now lifts up our dependence into Jesus' dependence on the Father. Because the Son descends so as to ascend to the right hand of the Father, so now all humanity is lifted up in the Son. The dependence that expresses our creaturehood is now an expression of our sonship in Christ. The Son makes us adopted sons and daughters.

Prayer, being in Christ, lifted into the life of the Trinity, cannot be about systems and practical tools, because using such things would be to rob God of his majesty and the freedom by which he chooses to encounter us. If there is anything practical to be done, it's to enter into prayer with the humility of Jesus: "Have the same mind in you which was in Christ Jesus who, though he was in the form of God, did not deem equality with God as something to be grasped at; rather, he emptied himself, taking the form of a slave, being born in human likeness. And it was thus that he humbled himself, obediently accepting death, death on a cross" (see Phil 2:5–8). Christ's humility is now our humility, and Christian prayer is about developing this disposition so that God in his great freedom can speak to us through personal prayer, Scripture, liturgy, and so on. Only through patient, humble listening do we enter into the prayer of Christ and allow him to lift us into the exchange of prayer that is the Father, Son, and Holy Spirit.

Our participation in Christ means to let go of judging the success of prayer. It means not letting our mood dictate the success of our prayer. Our success is in showing up and humbling ourselves before the Lord; God takes care of the rest. It is often only much later that we will see the secret working of grace, of our participation in Christ, and be able to judge it from afar. Prayer is simple: it's getting in touch with that part of ourselves, the core of our being which says, "God, I need you. Come to me."

CHAPTER 10

The Sacramentality of Discipleship

ONE OF THE MOST POWERFUL films I have seen is an Irish film called *Calvary*. The movie begins with a character named Father Lavelle sitting in a confessional. On the other side one can hear a penitent confessing all the ways he has been hurt by priests in the past. Then the penitent says, "I'm going to kill you, Father." He goes on to explain that if he were to kill a guilty priest, no one would think anything of it. People would figure that the priest deserved it. But, the man reasons, if he would kill an innocent priest, a good priest, then people would listen; then maybe they'd pay attention. The man proceeds to tell the priest that he will meet him at the beach one week from Sunday. The rest of the film involves Father Lavelle wrestling with what he should do. *Should he report the intended crime? Should he run away? Should he confront the man?*

The entire film is fascinating on a variety of levels. Obviously, it's a dramatic study of the abuse crisis in the Church. But it also has deeper themes that revolve around the nature of the priesthood and martyrdom. It powerfully portrays the nature of the priesthood as innocence offering itself for the guilty. Going even further, it shows that the essence of the Christian life is martyrdom: to be a Christian is to be oriented, in one way or another, toward martyrdom.

The martyrs of the Church are inspiring but also a little terrifying. We are inspired by their witness but can find it disturbing that some of them were eager to die for the faith. When we hear tales of martyrdom, we are often disturbed in two ways. We wonder, "How can someone be so eager to die?" and, "Will Jesus ask the same of me?"

The latter question especially bothers us because it's at the heart of Christian discipleship, which, as we said earlier, is a daily living out of the mystery of Christ's love for us and for the world. Most of us will not be eaten by lions, tortured by political opponents, or murdered because we are Catholic. But one of the central reasons we contemplate the martyrs and celebrate them in our tradition is because they express with their lives the ultimate form and principle of Christian discipleship—the cross. The highest form of Christian discipleship is the cross because we freely enter into death as Jesus did. Martyrdom is a clear witness to the cross. It's the supreme sacrifice, the ultimate icon of what Christian discipleship ought to look like. When we lose the guiding principle of martyrdom—letting Jesus' life be our way of life—we lose the heart of Christianity.

So, what exactly does this mean? First, we must take seriously what we've discussed so far—the sacramental worldview requires seeing the spiritual working through the physical, and the physical is the means through which we participate in the life of God. If we see and accept this, then we begin to see that Christianity is not a mere following of Jesus. Christian discipleship is not based on WWJD (What Would Jesus Do) moralism. That merely sees Jesus as a figure of the past, as someone to be imitated. But if we take Saint Paul's words seriously, that we are "in Christ," then Christian discipleship has a decisively sacramental character.

Christian discipleship involves opening our hearts to Jesus and allowing the pattern of his life to be lived out in us: his life, death, and resurrection. This is the sacramental vision of Christian discipleship in a nutshell. And it means preparing ourselves to die because death was the way Christ entered into his glory, and therefore our death is the means by which we share in his cross so as to share in his glory. So, let's explore what living Christ's life in us really means, and how it's the heart of all the victories and battles we face on the Christian journey. To see how this is possible, we will investigate four themes that encapsulate the totality of Christian life.

Christ Living in You

When given opportunities to live and learn about Christian virtue, we might feel alone and isolated. Some families attempt to live the Christian ideal without Catholic friends to lean on. Others are the only Catholics in their workplace, where persons easily get sucked into gossip, calumny, and office politics. But the good news is: no matter how much we feel alone, we are not in fact alone. Christ promises to be with us until the end of time (see Mt 28:20).

If we take seriously the sacramental worldview, we know that this promise isn't meant to be poetic, like saying, "His message lives on in us." No, when Jesus promises this, he means that he is with us in the most real sense possible, because he is in us and we are in him: "Abide in me as I abide in you" (Jn 15:4, NRSV).

To grow "in Christ"—to grow in our discipleship—is to grow in virtue. Because we live in the life of Christ, we share in a meaningful way in his virtues. In other words, if we are attempting to grow by not gossiping at the office, we do that in Christ. Christianity is not a "pick yourself up by your own bootstraps" religion. The love Christ demonstrates in the Gospels is ours in a real sense: the understanding he has for the woman at the well; the charity he shows to lepers desiring healing; the patience he exercises with the bumbling apostles; the depth of prayer he has with his Father; the selflessness he manifests on the cross. All of Christ's virtuous acts, attitudes, and behaviors are not just examples for us to imitate; we actually have access to them by means of our Baptism. The word in the Christian tradition that sums up this sharing in Christ's virtues is *grace*. Grace is a singular word that communicates the total gift we have by sharing in Christ's life.

The workings of grace are usually two-fold. First, grace brings a person to conversion. Conversion involves recognizing that Jesus really is "the Way, the Truth, and the Life" (see Jn 14:6). Only in Jesus are we saved, so conversion involves entering into his life to be ransomed from sin and death. How this works in the real, concrete, day-to-day is known as *justification*. Justification is the work of discipleship: we grow by sharing in Christ's life, allowing him to purify us from sin and let his virtues live in us more and more. Our efforts in this process are themselves a grace, because they are ultimately rooted in Christ and help work toward our justification. This process of justification is something we grow in for our entire lives.

The grace at work in justification is always given to us in the life of the Church. The sacraments, our acts of charity, the examples of the saints, the works of other Christians: these and many other activities are all means by which the singular and saving grace of Christ is made present to us to draw us into his life. This means that if we are attempting to grow in the virtue of caring for the poor, for example, we need not worry. Christ is acting in us to give us his heart for the poor, so that we can see him in them. If we need to grow in the virtue of patience, this is about slowing down to pray and asking Jesus to attune our heart to his, to allow his patience to become our patience. This is how we live in Christ and Christ lives in us. At every moment, Christ is using the circumstances and events of our lives to draw us more closely to himself.

Christ Crucified in You

If Christian discipleship is about living in Christ, then some of us might be asking ourselves, "How do I reconcile the sacramental vision of participation in the life of Christ with the burden of sin and temptation? If Christ is sinless and I am meant to live in him, what does that mean for me, a sinful human being?"

First, it's important to note that sin and temptation are not the same. Temptations are thoughts, feelings, and desires that arise in us and attempt to lead us to sin. Temptation in itself is not necessarily sin. Recall that Jesus himself was tempted by Satan in the desert, in his agony in the garden, in Peter's suggestion that Jesus should not be crucified, and in other events in the Gospels. As long as we fight against temptation with Jesus, we are not sinning. Still, temptation not only disturbs us but can overwhelm us, especially when it involves particular sins with which we struggle greatly.

A central motif in Jesus' response to temptation is that he does the will of his Father and in this he has victory. In Christ, our humanity has now overcome the snares of the devil, and freedom from sin is a real possibility. We know from our temptations that attempting to gain such freedom on our own is impossible. But in Christ, we now share in the battle against temptation. When we are tempted, we are in Christ in the desert, being tempted by the devil. We are in Christ in these moments insofar as we submit our will to the Father, gaining victory over sin and temptation. This means, then, that when we are tempted, we are actually not alone. Christ is in and with us, opening the merits of his victory against temptation for us to share in. It is in these moments, then, that we can say to Jesus, "Enter into this temptation, remove from me the desire to commit this particular sin." When tempted, it is also often advisable to pray for someone as a small act of charity. Sin wants to take, so the best way to let our hearts conform to Jesus' is to do a little act of charity, such as say a prayer for someone, to suffocate temptation's hold on us.

Yet, as humans we don't always succeed in the battle against temptation and, thus, sin is an element in our lives.

At times we give in to lesser venial sins and at others we sin mortally. Especially if it's a sin we have been battling for a while, it's easy to get discouraged and wonder, "Is Christ able to save me from this? Is his grace really at work? Why do I keep falling into the same sin over and over again?"

When we sin, we do hurt our relationship with God. But just because the relationship is hurt, it doesn't mean it's forever severed. Even when mortal sin breaks our communion with God, we know that our sin can be forgiven through confession. What's more, sin is not a place from which Christ is absent. Obviously, we ought not to sin in order to have a unique encounter with Christ. But we know that "he who knew no sin became sin for us" (see 2 Cor 5:21). He entered into the realm of sin and death in order to rescue us from its clutches. When we sin, Christ is already on a rescue mission to draw us back. Sin doesn't destroy our Baptism, and so Christ is still working to draw us back to him. Though our communion is severed in mortal sin, Christ enters into the depths of sin so as to unite it to his cross. Only when Christ takes our sin can we be redeemed and saved from its effects.

For his work to be effective, though, we also need to be receptive. We need to be humble and say, "Lord, here is my sin. I acknowledge it and ask you to save me from this sin and its effects that have injured my relationship with you and your Church." One of the hardest things for Christians to accept is that when we sin Christ still looks at us lovingly. He is always active, wanting to draw us deeper into the mystery of his life. Sin is not the last word; it becomes a means for a real encounter with grace. When sin is healed and forgiven, it's an encounter with the salvation offered us on the cross, in which grace transforms our sin into something good. Just as the cross of Jesus brought about salvation and the resurrection of the body, so too our sin can become transformed into a real grace in our lives, a deeper participation in Jesus' love and mercy, if we only open our hearts to it.

We may find it difficult to accept that God's grace from the cross is working in us when we sin. We sometimes see sin in such a horrific manner that we think it's not possible for Christ to be there. But the fact is, he has to be: not in the act of the sin, but in our soul, trying to inspire us to go to confession where he can touch the sin so as to heal it. This is the amazing mercy of God: that even in the worst of sins, insofar as we are willing to repent and reform our lives, Christ never gives up on us, but is always working, even in the darkness of our sin, so that we can move away from sin and into a deeper and more loving relationship with God.

One final note about sin and temptation. Discouragement and hopelessness are barometers of hope. By this I mean that when we allow despair, discouragement, and hopelessness to reign in the fight against sin, it's a sign that we need to retrain ourselves in hope. Hope is nothing more than recognizing that Christ is really active in us and in the Church. Through prayer and the sacramental life of the Church, we have real access to Jesus, and it's in these moments that we turn to him so we can see him anew.

Christ Suffering in You

The two greatest mysteries of life are suffering and death. Why do they exist? Why must we experience them? These two realities mark our lives perhaps more than anything else; they are two fundamental facts of life. Despite their universality, we naturally still ask, "Why me?" when intense suffering comes our way. Or we wonder why loved ones have to suffer and die. We struggle to understand this mystery, but it is impossible to fully grasp the meaning of suffering and death. The Book of Job gives testimony to this inability of ours to understand suffering. In response to Job's plight, God essentially says to him, "You're not God, so you cannot understand the purpose of this." Needless to say, such an answer can be deeply unsatisfying.

In Christianity, though, God begins to offer an answer to the problem of suffering and death. It's not an intellectual answer; rather, it's a Person, his Son, Jesus Christ. Christ enters willingly and with his whole being and life into suffering and death. In Christ we see that God does not try to eliminate suffering and death, bypass them, or ignore them. Christianity is a religion that enters fully into the human drama, leaving no stone of the human experience unturned. As fundamental human realities, suffering and death are no different; they can't be avoided, they can only be embraced. We could say, then, that participation is a two-way street. In Christ God participates—really and truly—in suffering and death. The cross of Christ is truly the heart of the Christian message because it's the heart of human tragedy, sin, and fallenness.

Let's break this down a bit more, because this is a profound fact of the Christian faith that needs to be internalized. When we think of suffering and death, it's rare to see them in a positive light. Because we've been trained in a worldview that sees suffering as something that lacks meaning or value, we struggle to see suffering and death as truly meaningful or even "good." This is why the cross is such a scandal: how can suffering and death be seen as the place where God's love is revealed if they serve no real purpose in human life? The heart of the Christian message is that God enters suffering and death and thereby makes them into a real good and a place of encounter with him. They are no longer meaning-less, they are meaning-full. The answer to the problem of suffering and death is not so much a rational justification, but the dwelling of a Presence, God himself in Christ. If Christ is there in the full reality of suffering and death, and we participate in his life, then when we are suffering and entering our final hours, Christ is really drawing us to him-self through his cross and resurrection. Suffering and death are perhaps some of the most intimate places of a real encoun-ter with the presence of God.

Thus, when we take seriously the sacramentality of the Christian life, suffering and death play a threefold role in our following of Christ. First, when we suffer and, eventually, when death comes our way, it's not something meaningless, but is a substantial and real meeting point with Christ. In these moments, the cross is really being lived out in us. In these moments, our bodies become real witnesses to our hope in Christ. Saint Paul recognizes this: "Christ will be magni-fied in my body, whether by life or by death" (Phil 1:20). It is the presence of Christ in suffering and death that imbues these mysteries with fullness of meaning—not through understanding, but through an encounter.

Second, suffering and death are redemptive. Recall once again that the Church is the universal sacrament of salvation, that Christ's death and resurrection bring salvation into our lives and into the world. Suffering and death, then, are the main means by which Christ effects his salvation in the world through the Church, making the Church, and all of us, sharers in his redeeming mission. We are co-redeemers and in our bodies are "filling up what is lacking in the afflictions of Christ on behalf of his body, which is the church" (Col 1:24). One of the key ways Jesus' redemption is both visible and effective in the world is through suffering and death: these are the means Jesus uses to make his cross present, not just in the life undergoing suffering, but as a sign of hope for those who need it, thereby witnessing to the Church, which is Christ's body and the place of redeemed humanity.

Finally, suffering and death are the center of Christian discipleship. If discipleship is going along Jesus' way—not only following his path, but allowing him to live out the pattern of his life in ours—then it's hard not to see these realities of suffering and death as the heart of the Christian life, as they are the heart of the life of Jesus. Recall earlier how we said that martyrdom is, in a way, the heart of Christian discipleship. Suffering and dying in hope become little martyrdoms, moments where we witness to Christ in the midst of what is senseless in the eyes of so many who lack hope. They are our greatest moments of weakness and powerlessness, yet they are precisely the moments when Christ works his grace in our lives the most, not just for our own good, but for the good of others. Such moments can be really effective for salvation because Christ wants to work through our suffering in order to draw others to him.

When we begin to see suffering and death through the lens of sacramentality—both as making visible what is invisible and as the key theme of participation—their role in the Christian life begins to make more sense. Sacramentality gives meaning and purpose to what we suffer and views it in the context of discipleship as a following of Christ's way. Thus, in a certain sense, a healthy view of sacramentality and discipleship is judged by how central a place we give to the cross. It is the standard of Christ's life, and therefore becomes the standard by which a Christian judges his or her life. Because the cross is at the heart of Christ's life, it's therefore the heart of the life of the disciple and of the Church. We would do well to keep this in mind: the cross is the place of hope, but we must go toward it with greater fervor.

Christ Loving in You

It was a unique event when Pope Benedict XVI published his first encyclical, called *Deus Caritas Est*—God is love. It was a first for an encyclical to devote itself solely to the nature and meaning of love. At the heart of the encyclical was the point that love is both *agape* and *eros*: self-giving love and desirous love. Both are needed, Pope Benedict said, for love to be real and authentic. *Eros* without *agape* would become a love that only takes for one's selfish needs, and *agape* without *eros* would lack desire and become harsh and demanding. For love to be love, it needs to be both at the same time.

The encyclical is well worth multiple reads, for there is always more to learn from it. But one key argument is that love—as uniquely revealed in the Gospels—is really and truly at the center of God's action in the Gospel. Now, the Pope is not speaking of a saccharine, sentimental view of love based solely on feelings. Rather, Christian love, as revealed by Christ, is found in what Saint John Paul II called "the law of the gift": we are most fully ourselves when we give ourselves away. To be human means to offer one's life so that another may live, and to do this with a deep desire for their good. This law is revealed through Christ's cross, where Jesus willingly chooses to offer himself for the good of humanity. This desirous sacrifice by Jesus gives us a window into the very heart of the Trinity: as Jesus offers himself on the cross, so too the three Persons of the Trinity offer themselves to each other in an eternal gift of love. So, if humanity is created in God's image and likeness, then the law of the gift is the most important form of Christian living. And Christian charity—loving as Christ loves—is possible because it's a real sharing in Jesus' love. It is through the grace of participating in his love that we are able to live Christ's way of love and make this love visible to the world.

You may be asking yourself, "What does this love look like? How do we participate in it and what does sharing in it look like?" To understand this, it's vital to look to the saints. The saints are icons of Christian charity, real windows into what Christ's love looks like. To put it differently, they are sacraments of Christian charity. By looking to them, we can really intuit and be inspired to Christian charity ourselves; by following their examples, we can embody Christ's love for the world.

To conclude this chapter, I'd like to share a moment from my time with the Missionaries of Charity—a congregation of religious sisters begun by Saint Teresa of Calcutta to serve the poor—and how this experience inspired me to be an instrument of Christian charity to others. I first met Christopher when he came into Gift of Love Hospice in San Francisco. He was dying of kidney failure. Christopher wasn't homeless but he lived in public housing and had a lifelong drinking problem and no friends or family. I was asked to clean Christopher when he arrived at the hospice from the hospital. Before I began, we chatted for a while. We bonded on the topic of hockey. He was a fan of the San Jose Sharks and I am a fan of the Canucks. After I finished cleaning him up, I asked him if he wanted to pray. He said, "No thanks. I don't believe in any of that God stuff." I replied, "No problem, have a good night's sleep," turned off his light, and went to pray for him myself.

Over the next couple weeks our relationship grew. Christopher's stomach had been terribly bloated but it was finally shrinking so we were able to get him into the shower. He needed help, so another care worker and I would help him. He was so happy in there. By the second day he simply grabbed the shower nozzle from our hands and just enjoyed the shower. Sometimes a shower would take an hour, because he was just so happy. One day, while another care worker and I were drying him off, he looked down at both of us intensely. He asked, "Why are you doing this?" I simply replied, "Because I love you and Jesus loves you" and continued to dry him off.

Two nights later, after I helped him get ready for bed, I noticed a change in his demeanor. He was happier and more peaceful. So, I asked him again, "Christopher, do you want to pray with me?" "Yes," he replied, "I'd like that very much."

We then prayed the Divine Mercy Chaplet together. While we were praying, I got an overwhelming inspiration from the Holy Spirit that was too powerful to ignore. The inspiration was clear: to ask him if he wanted to be baptized. And so I did. Then I explained to him what Baptism is. "Oh!" he replied. "I would love to have that. I want God's love." We quickly called Deacon Ben over and he performed the Baptism right away with me as the godfather. The look of peace on Christopher's face was unforgettable. Christopher died two days later.

Loving Christopher with a smile, participating spiritually in his sufferings, and proposing the Gospel in all I said and did with him was not my own work. It was possible because just like all of the baptized, I was living in Christ, and, ultimately, it's Christ himself who brings others to his love and salvation. When we allow ourselves to participate in the life of God, God works through us and manifests himself to others through us. This is the heart of sacramentality. To live sacramentality means that Christian charity effuses out of us, often without our quite noticing it. Living Christian charity is one of the preeminent ways in which the sacramental worldview is lived, because it is nothing other than making the love of God visible. When charity reveals God to others, it begins to propose a question to the human heart. There was never one moment when Christopher asked, "Why am I suffering?" but he did ask, "Why am I loved?" The radical nature of Christian charity is one of the quickest ways to propose the Gospel to the world, and the most direct way to make Christ visible through us. That is sacramental living at its fullest.

Conclusion

Where Do We Go from Here?

YOU MAY HAVE WONDERED AS you read this book, "If we are discussing sacramentality so much, why aren't we discussing the seven sacraments?" While it's true that the sacraments have been mentioned, I did not write an entire chapter on them for two reasons. First, I did not want anyone to get hung up on the term "sacrament" and think of it as only referring to the seven instituted sacraments. Second, when we did talk about the sacraments, they were seen as an integrated whole within the wider sacramental vision of the Christian life.

Hopefully by now you've learned and internalized that the term "sacrament," while never excluding the centrality of the seven sacraments, has much broader usage than what we first realized. This is a vision of sacramentality that the Church Fathers and medieval Christians understood with great depth. And in recent times—especially through the efforts of the Second Vatican Council— the Church has attempted to revitalize this deeper sacramental vision. Of course, the seven sacraments are definitely the most effective forms through which Jesus communicates his life to us. They are the source and summit of the Christian life. They are the lifeblood of the Church. And most of us already know this. We know the seven sacraments, what they are signs of, and how they communicate the grace of Jesus' life to us. Yet, we can be so unaware of the reality that's been discussed throughout: in everything we say, do, and think as Christians, we are participating in the life of Christ.

When attending baptisms, you may have noticed that the priest gives a newly lit baptismal candle to the godparents as a sign that the child has now been enlightened by Christ. To be enlightened means to be able to see the world anew, with fresh eyes: to have faith, as we have said, means to see things through Jesus' eyes. The purpose of this book, similarly, has been to enlighten your soul so you can see the vast truth of our faith: to be a Christian means to be *in Christ*. For this reason, we've purposely avoided more practical discussions. We are already oversaturated with the practical; we are so tempted to want to hear the three steps we need to take. But focusing on enlightening and being immersed in Christ moves us away from a pragmatic view of the faith. This avoidance of practicality is not to denounce the practical life. Rather, it is intended to help bring us back into a healthy balance between the enlightening and the practical. The purpose of Christian living is to give priority to being enlightened, to seeing the world properly. Through prayer, sacraments, learning, and Christian virtue, we allow God to enlighten our minds so we can see reality more clearly and be better poised to act with the heart of Christ.

Of course, despite all that has been said, you may be asking the question: exactly how do I live this out? I hesitate to offer an answer on a personal level, because, as mentioned above, we too easily want a pragmatic solution instead of allowing grace to be mediated to us and to transform us. But the life of faith does include action and works. As Saint James says, "faith of itself, if it does not have works, is dead" (Jas 2:17). There are active responses that are the fruit of grace, the working out of our justification to draw us into Christ. I would like to offer a few examples that are not by any means exhaustive, but may serve as guideposts to foster our formation by the sacramental worldview.

So often in my pastoral ministry, I hear from young couples who want to have their child baptized that they would practice the faith more, but they don't know any other Catholics. The feeling of being alone in the faith is often one of the biggest obstacles to living it more intentionally. This is why Jesus instituted the Church, to meet this human need that he placed in us. The Catholics we have around us are often the people through whom Christ works to draw us to himself. They are members of the Church and therefore are the means by which Christ mediates his presence to us in a variety of ways. It is important, therefore, to at least attempt to seek out Christian communion. I use the word "communion" over "community" because the Church is more than a community and her bonds are deeper than what community often provides.

Having good Christian friendships can be a special help for everyone. For young people, the Church's communion becomes the means by which they often discern their vocation. Families develop friendships and supports as they work to raise their kids in a world not always friendly to Christians. The retired, the single, the elderly, the immigrant, the poor: everyone has a place and purpose, and all can encounter Christ more totally by seeking bonds of friendship in the Church's great communion. The Church's communion also gives us a support network of people with whom we can discuss living out our faith. Remember, the sacramental vision is meant to build upon the natural needs and structures of life. So those needs for friendships in which there are people to encourage and correct us are vital to the Christian faith because they're vital to life.

The best way to form community is around the liturgy of the Church, especially her festivities. By celebrating a particular feast together, being intentional about preparing food, choosing entertainment, and setting aside a time, living according to the Church's liturgy creates a bond of communion among us that seeps over beyond the liturgy into our lived out experience.

One of my favorite ways to live this is to celebrate the little extra privileges of the Church's year. As we know, it is the common practice for Catholics to give up meat on Fridays as a penance to unite ourselves with Christ's sacrifice. But when a solemnity falls on a Friday, that law is to be ignored for the sake of the solemnity. So, on the Solemnity of the Sacred Heart—which always falls on a Friday—I often gather friends together for a big steak dinner. We sit and enjoy our meal, and discussions around faith, friendship, and life's meaning naturally come up. Finding ways to do this intentionally, inviting other Catholics into living out the liturgy, is a fantastic way for us to mediate Christ to others, to allow others to mediate Christ to us, and thereby allow ourselves to be more deeply formed by a sacramental vision that touches all of space and time.

I want to focus on the liturgy a bit more because it really is one of the principal ways Christ forms us in the sacramental vision. In fact, an unspoken principle in this entire book has been the idea that symbols matter. Oil, water, bread, wine, words: all of these are essential to the sacramental vision. The liturgy should be rich, not poor, in symbol because each symbol is a means through which God communicates his very life to the Church. Thus, the way we celebrate liturgy can be incredibly formative in allowing Christ to imbue our souls with a deeper sense of sacramentality.

But it's no secret that there have been a lot of debates in the Church around liturgy. To put it rather simplistically, some people think that we should, essentially, be able to make the liturgy of the Church into whatever we want: we can use different forms of bread; change the prayers of institution at Eucharist; for some, perhaps even forego the Mass. Then there is the other camp who think that any reform of liturgy is anathema, and that we should just go back to the way things were prior to the Second Vatican Council. But in the midst of all this, with the understanding that symbols matter in the life of the Church, we can grow to allow the liturgy to form us more deeply if we are open to the depth of symbolism that the liturgy has always held. Yes, it is true that abuses have happened over the last fifty years, and yes, it is true that some liturgies have become banal instead of pointing us toward the transcendent beauty of God. But instead of allowing our discussions surrounding liturgy to become combative, we can take a more subtle approach in which we work to reconnect our current liturgical practices to the Church's tradition.

Cardinal Ratzinger (Pope Emeritus Benedict XVI) is a noted promoter of this more subtle and careful approach. He encouraged it because he felt that the reforms of the Council were imposed in a bureaucratic and inorganic fashion. In his opinion, a similar bureaucratic imposition on liturgical reform would create too much division and only escalate the liturgical wars instead of bringing about a healthy and charitable dialogue. This means that, going forward, reform really needs to be organic because that is how the Church has always functioned. It also means that everyone's approach to liturgy must acknowledge the value of our liturgical tradition, and see and promote important gestures in the liturgy that help build up the sacramental worldview.

For priests, this could mean small matters like celebrating Mass *ad orientem*—facing the East. Looking at the idea of *ad orientem* from the perspective of this book, the symbol never means that the priest turns his back to the people. Rather, it is a sign that the People of God are going to the throne of the Lamb together. It builds up in us the idea that the Church is a pilgrim people on this earth, journeying toward the Lord. Another possibility is one the Second Vatican Council called for: the inclusion of chant and Latin in the Mass.

If we can be open to such practices and see that the Mass is not about taste but about God working in us, then we can see them as symbolically important in helping draw us into God's life. They form us so that we become God's people and see the heavenly liturgy as our goal, in which we already participate in anticipation here on earth. The whole point of the sacramental worldview is that God uses signs and symbols to make present heavenly realities, and these are some of the essential ways that can happen in liturgy. This means that our discussions around liturgy, rather than being combative, ought to open our hearts to the tradition that God has worked through and help us see how it has formed his people in the past so that these same signs and symbols can form the People of God in the Church today.

Finally, if we want to embrace the sacramental worldview, we really must embrace the importance and centrality of signs and symbols not just liturgically but also culturally, artistically, and so on. Symbol is what guarantees mystery, and mystery, as we learned at the beginning of this book, is at the heart of the sacramental worldview. It helps us see that there is a deeper meaning to everything, more than just an analytical breaking down to the most basic elements. Not only does this help us to see the mystery behind all things, but it helps us grow in awe and wonder.

Awe and wonder: these are the virtues we need to build in order to live out the sacramental worldview. We can grow in awe and wonder by recognizing our dependence on God and allowing it to help us see the whole world as a gift. Think about a time you received a gift that had intention and purpose behind it. Consider how this gave the item a meaning beyond what you would normally find in it. This is true of all creation: it is all gift. God is the one who gives us all of creation out of love for us. Thus, all things have a deeper meaning. We simply need the eyes to see, which means we must embrace our dependence on God. For when we accept the fact that we are dependent, we are positioned to receive all things as gifts from God, and that is the beginning of wonder.

Once we have wonder toward all things, we begin to see all things—not just the created world in general, but the life, tradition, and liturgy of the Church, with all its intricate symbols and meanings—as essential to viewing the world sacramentally. We begin to be in awe and wonder before the liturgical gestures and symbols, before the teachings of the Church, before the beauty of a life of saintly virtue. In all this we will finally *see* the world as Christ intended us to see it: as a sign, a symbol of his love, and as the place of encounter with the God who created us.

Reader's Guide

CHAPTER 1

Mystery and Sacrament

In the first chapter, we learn the deep meaning of the word "mystery" and its fourfold meaning in the Christian tradition. Learning the depth of this term opens us to the deeper meaning of the word "sacrament," and how its meaning and implication for us as Christians goes far beyond the seven sacraments we receive.

1. Ponder the contemporary "icon" on the cover of the book. Do you see different aspects of the concept of mystery at play? Look for what conceals and what makes present salvation as well as how the icon draws you to a deeper sense of your participation in Christ.

2. The sense of sacrament as presented in this chapter and in the rest of the book is much broader than you might be used to. What do you find new or difficult about this concept of sacramentality?

3. One of the core themes of the book is that sacramentality is central to the total Christian vision of the world. Discuss how you think you might evangelize people with this in mind. What are some ways we could proclaim Jesus to others while keeping sacramentality in mind?

CHAPTER 2

Participation in Christ

To be in Christ is to live the life of participation. Our Baptism makes possible Christ living in us and we in him. This is at the heart of the sacramental worldview. This real closeness with Christ means that God uses our history, our life events, and the whole material world to draw near to us. In this chapter, we learn that the sacramental worldview reveals to us three key things about seeing the world as Christians.

1. God works through his creation. Why is the physical stuff of creation so important to encounter God? Have there been moments in life where an event made you more aware of God's presence? What were the things, people, places that were at play?

2. The physical is the means by which we encounter the spiritual. If to have faith is to see things through the eyes of Christ, what does that mean to you? How do we develop the spiritual vision to see the deeper reality of things and to see God? What have you found to be a

hindrance to developing that spiritual vision? What do you find helpful?

3. The whole crux of the sacramental worldview is that we see God through his creation because we participate in the life of Christ. Participation is the key word. Reread the quote by Saint Hilary on page 31. Break down the passage and discuss the deeper meaning of participation as described in the quote.

CHAPTER 3
Modernism: The Obstacle to the Sacramental Worldview

Modernism undermines the very substance and meaning of the sacramental worldview. In essence, it opposes the basis of the Christian worldview by denying that God can interact with the world and that God works through the world to make himself known to us and save us. Regardless of our background, modernism is part of our everyday life; it is the presupposition we work out of all the time, and it makes Christianity difficult to embrace and live today.

1. What are some ways mentioned in this chapter that modernism undermines Christianity? Can you think of ways not mentioned that modernism undermines the Christian vision?

2. If modernism is the denial of the ability of God to work in the world, in what places in your life have you allowed this to be true? How can you counteract this

way of thinking and acting, not just theologically, but in a lived way?

3. How can we best approach non-Christians influenced by modernism, not only through arguments but through our way of living? Considering that the starting point for most people is the idea that God might exist but has no real impact in the world and leaves us to our own devices, how can we propose the faith to people anew?

CHAPTER 4

The Church as the Place of Faith

The Church is the "place" of faith, meaning that faith is fundamentally a gift given by God rather than simply personal assent. The Church is the necessary place where we encounter Christ. But we also recognize the word "church" can have a lot of negative connotations, not only for non-Catholics but even for many Catholics.

1. What is the Church? Is it just the institution? Just the clergy? The magisterium? What role do the laity and all the baptized have in the Church?

2. Reflect on the definition from the Second Vatican Council that the Church is the "universal sacrament of salvation." Why is the Church necessary for making Christ present to the world?

3. If faith is a gift we can only receive through the Church, what implications does that have? How can

we share this truth with others without alienating them?

4. Why is the Church necessary for a deep, abiding, participatory communion with Jesus? How does this happen in our lives through the Church?

CHAPTER 5
The Church as Communion

In this chapter we discuss the features, contours, and mission of the Church, including apostolic succession, the sacraments, and the mission of the Church to make the salvation of Christ visible and effective in the world. The Church, then, is the means by which we really participate in the life of Christ. Thus, it's important to talk about some of these features so we can really internalize the nature and mission of the Christian in and through the Church.

1. What does it mean when the Second Vatican Council (*Lumen Gentium*) said that the Church is the "universal sacrament of salvation"?

2. Just as the Church can be a sacrament of salvation, her members can also become a sort of anti-sacrament by interfering with the process of making Christ and his salvation visible to others. How can we avoid being an "anti-sacrament"?

3. The heart of our life in the Church as Christians is to receive grace and then go out to others. Brainstorm some ways that you can go out and bring Christ and his

salvation to others, as well as ways you can offer opportunities to people to come in and experience what it
means to be "in Christ."

Chapter 6
The Marian Stance

Our section on the Church in this book concludes with a
reflection on Mary. She is the archetype of the Church, the
one toward whom we look in order to understand what the
Church is. A need in the Church and thus in our own lives is
to be Marian, to participate in her open stance toward the
Son. In order for the Church to fully realize her mission, and
for us to live that mission, we must become more Marian.

1. Pragmatism is a mindset that can strongly govern our
   lives. How have you seen this at work in your own life?
   Do you tend to think, "What do I need to do to get
   holier? What plan or project must I follow toward holiness?" Mary teaches us that the heart is not first oriented toward doing, but rather toward being. To be
   Marian is to be more receptive. What does receptivity
   look like in our relationship with God?

2. Contemplation is at the heart of Mary's attitude. She
   "pondered these things in her heart" is a phrase Saint
   Luke uses repeatedly in his Gospel. Contemplation
   means to always be ready to listen to God. Yet life is
   often the opposite: we are quick to make judgments and
   slow to ponder, and we lack the silence to be attuned to
   the voice of God. What does contemplation look like

in prayer, liturgy, and in living out your vocation? How can you, your family, and your parish be more contemplative?

3. Mary, as Mother of the Church, pondered everything in her heart for the sake of the whole Church. She holds these things in her heart for our sake and makes the mysteries of salvation known to us through her heart. And her heart, which gives freely, is meant to be ours as well. What does a Marian heart look like in our own Christian vocation?

CHAPTER 7
Liturgy as Living Out Christ's Life

In this chapter, we enter into the more concrete aspects of the sacramental worldview, where we see how our participation in Christ is lived out. For the Christian, liturgical life is the heart of our participation in Christ. It feeds and nourishes us for the mission of making the salvation of Christ known to the world. To integrate the centrality of liturgy in our lives, therefore, is absolutely vital for embracing the sacramental worldview.

1. The importance of ritual is so often dismissed. Both Catholics and non-Catholics can see ritual as something magical or unnecessary. Yet ritual is part of being human. Do you struggle with the ritual of the Church? How does the sacramental worldview help you in this struggle? What could you say to someone who struggles with the ritual aspect of the Church's

liturgical life in order to help them see that it is actually beautiful and central to being human?

2. Our Baptism is not just a one-time ritual where we receive the saving grace of Christ through water; it is a sacrament always active within us, the gateway to being immersed into Jesus' life. What does the gift of Baptism open up for us through the Church's liturgy? What does participation in Christ's saving mysteries through liturgy look like?

3. In the liturgical year, the rhythms of our lives are lifted up into the seasons of Christ's ministry and saving death and resurrection. What are some ways you can live out the liturgical year at home so as to accentuate the reality of this participation more clearly? Are there things you could do to invite those who don't know Christ to encounter him through these activities?

CHAPTER 8

The Holy Mass: Christ Glorifies the Father Through the Church

The sacraments exist for the sake of mission, and the Mass is the sacrament *par excellence* that nourishes us and enables us to go out for mission. Thus, it is vital that we understand what Christ is doing in us so we can bring Christ to the world.

1. Pope Francis speaks of a "spiritual navel-gazing" that can happen with regard to the sacraments. Are you eas-

ily tempted to emphasize the "for me" element of the sacraments and to forget the fact that they build us up to lay down our lives for our friends? How do the sacraments help us to live for others?

2. We can easily look at Christian ritual and see it as empty and ineffective. This is often because we do not allow the ritual to affect and change us. How do you live your life as a witness for or against the saving works of Christ? How can you better allow the Church's liturgy to transform you? How can this way of thinking inspire your day-to-day living?

CHAPTER 9

The Mystery of Christian Prayer

Prayer is the vital living-out of our Baptism. It is the place of our essential, day-to-day encounters with Jesus. In prayer we are nourished in a loving relationship with the Holy Trinity and given everything we need to live out our Christian mission every day.

1. How is your prayer life right now? Reflect on this for a time in view of what you read in this chapter.

2. As you grow in embracing the sacramental worldview, how might this change your understanding of prayer?

3. Many different ways of prayer are suggested in this chapter that come from the Church's lived experience. Was there one you hadn't heard of before that you might consider adding to your prayer life?

CHAPTER 10

The Sacramentality of Discipleship

At the heart of the sacramental worldview is the idea that Christ is always at work; that we always participate in him; and that the spiritual is at work in the physical, in the concrete. Discipleship is living out the fact that Christ is really and truly encounterable in all things every day.

1. Taking seriously the idea of sacramentality, what does the phrase "the heart of Christian discipleship is martyrdom" mean? What might that look like?

2. We so often look for blessings—and by this we mean the good things of life—but we forget that our faith includes participation in the suffering and Cross of Christ. How does discipleship embrace this aspect of our faith? Why is this essential for sacramental living?

3. What might living the "law of the gift" look like in your life? How might you do these things in, with, and through Christ?

Concluding Questions

1. Having now read the book, does evangelization look different to you? Do you see some ways you might incorporate sacramentality more thoroughly into your proclamation of the Gospel? Brainstorm some ways this book can inspire new forms of evangelization.

2. Evangelization involves meeting people where they're at. Modernism is where many people are existentially, and it creates a barrier to the experience of Christ. How might you talk to someone who has fallen into the idea of modernism without perhaps even realizing it? How can we develop new forms of apologetics to help people open their hearts to the Gospel? Which experiences of beauty, truth, and goodness could open more hearts to Christ?

About the Cover Art

This work of sacred art is pulling from the tradition of iconography to lead the viewer into a prayerful encounter with the person of Jesus Christ.

The artist of the image on the book cover sought to illustrate the sacramental worldview as a doorway to a rich understanding of the created world. Rooted in a disposition of wonder and awe, the story of this contemporary "icon" begins in what is not visible. The veil we pass through on the jacket design, though not visible in the image itself, represents how the natural world reveals to us an understanding of the spiritual world.

In the icon, the birds of the air and fish of the sea amid the variety of vegetation represent the diversity and abundance of the world God created in Genesis. The sun and moon represent God's presence and authority in the world, as well as his being the Alpha and Omega of Revelation. The face on the sun symbolizes God's presence in creation, which illumines the day; the face on the moon represents God's presence in the body of Christ, God's people who receive his light.

In the figure of Jesus, the Divine Master, we see how Christ is alive and active in the world around us, inviting us into his life. Rather than posing as a distant, impersonal ruler of creation, Christ stands with his body and gaze oriented toward us—toward humanity, with whom he shares the depths of the human experience—in order to enter into relationship with us. Jesus is clothed in the crimson of sacrifice and wrapped in the white purity of his desire to give us himself. With his right hand, he offers the inseparable bond and unity of the Trinity. In the other, he holds open God's word, revealing the meaning of the Father's plan for us in Scripture, which we receive in and through the Church. The peacock, the pagan symbol of eternity later Christianized as a symbol of the resurrection, draws near to the figure of Jesus to also show how time and eternity come together in Christ.

All of the action in the image takes place within the mantle of Mary, Mother of the Church. The figure of Mary in the icon offers her Son to us with her arms opened wide. Her mantle shaped like a chalice presents the Christ Child holding out the word of God and cloaked again in the crimson of sacrifice, symbolizing wine turned to Blood in the Eucharist. Mary and Jesus are wearing teal, the color of the dawn that intercedes between heaven and earth, representing the connection between Jesus our Redeemer and Mary our intercessor and mediatrix with her Son.

The focus on Jesus and Mary in the icon highlights how participation in Christ and the Mass ignites in us a liturgy of life in which we unite our own life with Christ's sacrifice, consecrating this world and all that we experience to him. With Mary, Mother of Christ and our Mother, we are led through the waters of our Baptism back through the veil to communicate Jesus to a world thirsting for all that is true, good, and beautiful.

BOOKS & MEDIA

The Daughters of St. Paul operate book and media centers at the following addresses. Visit, call, or write the one nearest you today, or find us at www.paulinestore.org.

CALIFORNIA
3908 Sepulveda Blvd, Culver City, CA 90230   310-397-8676
3250 Middlefield Road, Menlo Park, CA 94025   650-562-7060

FLORIDA
145 S.W. 107th Avenue, Miami, FL 33174   305-559-6715

HAWAII
1143 Bishop Street, Honolulu, HI 96813   808-521-2731

ILLINOIS
172 North Michigan Avenue, Chicago, IL 60601   312-346-4228

LOUISIANA
4403 Veterans Memorial Blvd, Metairie, LA 70006   504-887-7631

MASSACHUSETTS
885 Providence Hwy, Dedham, MA 02026   781-326-5385

MISSOURI
9804 Watson Road, St. Louis, MO 63126   314-965-3512

NEW YORK
115 E. 29th Street, New York City, NY 10016   212-754-1110

SOUTH CAROLINA
243 King Street, Charleston, SC 29401   843-577-0175

VIRGINIA
1025 King Street, Alexandria, VA 22314   703-549-3806

CANADA
3022 Dufferin Street, Toronto, ON M6B 3T5   416-781-9131

¡También somos su fuente para libros,
videos y música en español!